LOUISIANA TROOPS

1720 - 1770

by WINSTON DE VILLE

CLEARFIELD

Copyright © 1965 by Winston De Ville
All Rights Reserved.
Permission for reproduction in any form
may be obtained from the publisher.

Originally published
Fort Worth, Texas, 1965

Reprinted for
Clearfield Company, Inc. by
Genealogical Publishing Co., Inc.
Baltimore, Maryland
1994, 1999

International Standard Book Number: 0-8063-4921-2

Made in the United States of America

TO HELEN

CONTENTS

Preface   xi

Louisiana Troops   3

Appendix, Louisiana Officers, 1692-1776   122

Map of Mississippi and Ohio Valleys   137

Map of Louisiana   138

PREFACE

The following list of French soldiers of 18th-century Louisiana was compiled from document number AC, D2C, 54:1, in the Library of Congress. Originally written in French and only partially alphabetized, the entries have been translated and arranged to be of maximum value to researchers.

The uses of this book are obvious. The genealogist will find the names and brief service records of many early Louisiana ancestors. The historian may choose to examine the pages for some details of military organization, military strength and growth, discipline, and other topics relating to the French military troops in Louisiana. Particularly useful to the historian will be the list of officers included as an appendix and indexed in the Library of Congress D2C, 59:1-81, I and II. The originals of both lists are in the **Archives des Colonies** in Paris.

The knowledgeable researcher will quickly observe that this seemingly exhaustive list fails to include names of certain men whom we know served France in Louisiana. For this, the officials offered no excuse—nor can we, except to say that the French were poor record-keepers and such haphazardness in "official" business was common.

This project was begun in the winter of 1962 in Baton Rouge, although most of the real work was completed at Montrose on Mobile Bay from June, 1963, to July, 1964, with the valuable help of Herbert Shipp of Mobile. Final drafts were made in the Vieux Carré in New Orleans, January, 1965.

Winston De Ville

January 8, 1965

LOUISIANA TROOPS, 1720-1770

LOUISIANA TROOPS —:— 1720-1770

ABERT, JEAN
Died at the hospital, January 3, 1754, Gamont's Company.

ABRIEL, PIERRE

AGÉ, LOUIS

AGUILLE, ANTOINE
Discharged March 31, 1761. See the roll for the same year, folio 3.

AIRAULT, RENÉ
Cadet soldier. Went to France on the royal flute, the Fortune January 1, 1759. See the roll of June 1, 1760, folio 1.

ALAIN GUILLAUME
Died October 28, 1745, Le Blanc's Company.

ALBERT, PELAGEON PETAIL

ALBIN NICOLAS
With half-pay according to a decision of May 16, 1764, sent to the Bureau des Invalidese the same day.

ALBOT, PIERRE
Discharged September 15, 1763. folio 13.

ALEXANDRE, LOUIS
Discharged August 1, 1761. See the roll of the same year, folio 36.

ALLEMAND, CLAUDE
Died October 23, 1751.

ALLEMANDÉ, JOSEPH (sic)
Died October 3, 1751.

ALLIAUME, JOSEPH
Drowned in the sinking of the Pere de Famille February 17, 1770, returning to France.

ALLIOT, JACQUES
Discharged August 10, 1754 with one-half pay, decision of August 10, 1764, sent the same day to the Bureau des Invalides.

ALORGE, PIERRE
Sergeant. Died November 19, 1757, Du Tillet's company.

AMANDOX, PIERRE ALEXIS
Died at New Orleans August 27, 1768. Roll of January 1 1763, folio 35.

AMON, JEAN

ANCART, PIERRE JOSEPH
Discharged September 15, 1763. Roll of January 1, 1763, folio 21.

ANCELIN, FRANCOIS
Died August 27, 1755, company of Mazam.

ANDOUE, CLAUDE
Discharged September 15, 1763. Roll of January 1, 1763, folio 1.

ANDRÉ, JACQUES
Deserted June 15, 1756.

ANDRÉ, JEAN BAPTISTE

ANDRÉ, NICOLAS
Died August 25, 1751.

ANDRÉ, PIERRE

ANDRIEUX, JEAN

ANDRY, LOUIS ANTOINE
Discharged July 1, 1756.

ANGENOIL, DENIS
Discharged September 15, 1763. Roll of January 1, 1763, folio 1.

ANJOURA, JACQUES ANTOINE
Sergeant. Discharged in Louisiana July 28, 1762. Half-pay at 12 livres per month payable at Arles, according to a decision of September 22, 1763, sent to the Bureau des Invalides October 12, 1763.

ANTHEAUME, LOUIS
Died January 17, 1750.

ANJOURS, JACQUES ANTOINE

ANOX, CLAUDE
Went to France on the Thetis April 14, 1770.

ANSELIN, PIERRE
Discharged May 1, 1750.

ANTOINE, FRANCOIS
Discharged September 15, 1763. Roll of January 1, 1763, folio 2.

ARBELAT, PIERRE
Died September 25, 1750.

ARBRE, MICHEL

ARBRE or ARBER, MICHEL
Discharged February 6, 1770, at half-pay of 4 livres, 20 sols per month, according to a decision of November 1, 1771.

ARBLARD, CLAUDE
Deserted in 1750.

ARBONNE, ANTOINE

ARBUS, PIERRE

LOUISIANA TROOPS —:— 1720-1770

ARCIS, JEAN ALLIVIER
Died September 30, 1751.

ARDILLY, LOUIS
Discharged September 15, 1763. Roll of January 1, 1763, folio 23.

ARGADAN, PIERRE JOSEPH FRANCOIS
With half-pay, according to a decision of April 4, 1764, sent to the Bureau des Invalides on April 5, 1764. Discharged September 15, 1763.

ARGILLIER, ETIENNE
Executed by firing squad (passé par les armes), September 6, 1751.

ARIAS, JEAN
Discharged September 15, 1763. Roll of January 1, 1763, folio 2.

ARLAY, JEAN BAPTISTE
Half-pay of 6 livres, according to a decision of March 22, 1765, sent to the Bureau des Invalides.

ARLOT, JEAN
Went to France on the Samson October 1, 1769. Roll of January 1, 1763, folio 44.

ARMAND, FRANCOIS
Discharged March 1, 1765. Roll of January 1, 1763, folio 32.

ARNAL, JACQUES MARIE
Discharged May 1, 1750.

ARNAUD, HUGHES
Deserted July 4, 1756.

ARNOULT, PIERRE
Died August 3, 1720. The certificate is at the Bureau des Invalide.

ARNOUX, CLAUDE
Fusilier. Discharged August 20, 1770, at half-pay of 4 livres, 10 sols per month, according to a decision of October 8, 1770.

ARTUAD, PIERRE
Deserted September 3, 1757, and condemned by contumacy July 24, 1758, to be executed before a firing squad. See the roll of June 1, 1760, folio 12.

ASSASSIN, PIERRE JOSEPH
Died in June, 1758. See the roll of January 1, 1760, folio 4.

AUBERT, JOSEPH

AUBERTIN, FRANCOIS
Drowned in the river while ascending to Pointe Coupee, Mar. 5, 1754. Murat's company.

AUDIN, FRANCOIS
Discharged September 15, 1763. Roll of January 1, 1763, folio 10.

AUDIN, JEAN
Died at the hospital July 2, 1759. See the roll of June 1, 1760, folio 9.

AUDRAN, FRANCOIS
Died at Natchez, July 7, 1756, Grandpre's company.

AUGER, LOUIS
Deserted February 5, 1739.

AUGERON, JOSEPH

AUPERT, JACQUES

AURIQUE, ANTOINE

AULARD, FRANCOIS

AULARD, FRANCOIS
Discharged September 15, 1763. Roll of January 1, 1763, folio 20.

AUMONT, RENÉ
Discharged September 15, 1763. Roll of January 1, 1763, folio 22.

AUPIN, CHARLES
Discharged September 15, 1763. Roll of January 1, 1763, folio 18.

AUSSART, JACQUES
Discharged September 10, 1756.

AUVRAY, JACQUES
Died at the hospital 25 December, 1755, Macarthy's company. His death certificate, drawn May 8, 1764, was sent June 5, 1764, to M. Mitoyen, order of the King's music.

AUVRAY, NICOLAS

AUVRAY, NICOLAS
Corporel. Discharged February 6, 1770 at half-pay of 6 livres per month, according to a decision of April 28, 1770.

AVIGNY, FRANCOIS
Discharged February 6, 1770. De Vaugine's company.

LOUISIANA TROOPS —:— 1720-1770

BACHAT, NICOLAS
Died at the Balize December 13, 1766, roll of January 1, 1763, folio 33.

BACHART or BACHAT, NICOLAS

BACHE, CLAUDE

BAFFÉ, CLAUDE
Went to Santo Domingo July 22, 1763 on the frigate Aigrette, roll of January 1, 1763, folio 3.

BAILLY, JEAN

BAILLY, JOSEPH
With half-pay of 6 livres per month according to a decision of April 4, 1764, sent to the Bureau des Invalides April 5, 1764.

BAILLY, LOUIS
Died October 10, 1764, roll of January 1, 1763, folio 29.

BAILLOT, PIERRE

BAILLOT, SIMON

BALLE, JEAN
Deserted June 19, 1755.

BANCE, PIERRE
Died October 16 1751.

BANDÉ, JEAN
Discharged August 1, 1764, roll of January 1, 1763, folio 27.

BAPTISTE
Negro servant of Sieur Destour. Drowned in the sinking of the Pere de Famille February 17, 1770.

BAPTISTE, FRANCOIS
died at the hospital June 25, 1758. See the roll of June 1, 1760, folio 3.

BARBAY, LOUIS

BARBET, FRANCOIS
Discharged May 1, 1750.

BARBIER, ANDRÉ JOSEPH
Discharged September 15, 1763, roll of January 1, 1763, folio 2.

BARBIER, CLAUDE ANTOINE
Drowned while descending from Natchez October 2, 1754, Macarty's company.

BARBIER, LOUIS ANTOINE

BARBIER, PIERRE
Died April 6, 1734. Certificate at the bureau.

BARBOTIN, MATHURIN

BARDON, JEAN
Discharged September 15, 1763, roll of January 1, 1763, folio 13.

BARON ANTOINE

BAROU, ANDRÉ
Deserted in October, 1754.

BARRE PIERRE
Died August 18, 1755, D'Erneville's company.

BARRIERE, JEAN
Dismissed (chassé) July 23, 1769, roll of January 1, 1763, folio 36.

BARRY, CHARLES
Deserted November 20 1756.

BARTHE, ANTOINE
Died at the residence of M. Marault April 12, 1768, roll of January 1, 1763, folio 36.

BARTHELEMY, ANTOINE

BARUTEL, BLAIZE
Disbanded (licencié) at Havre, see the general roll of February 22, 1761 folio 7. Sent from this port, (by) order of the King dated July 10, 1761, to petition for his discharge (papers) which were stolen from him in Paris on Madelaine Street.

BASLE, NICOLAS
Deserted February 5, 1739.

BASQUE, PIERRE
Died at New Orleans November 21, 1769. See the copy of a list sent by M. Daubenton (sic) concerning the sinking of the Pere de Famille and the roll of January 1, 1763, folio 34.

BASTIEN, FRANCOIS
Discharged March 31, 1761. See the roll of the detached compagnies franches, folio 3. Died at Pointe Coupee June 5, 1767, roll of January 1, 1763, folio 5.

LOUISIANA TROOPS —:— 1720-1770

BASTIEN, ANTOINE
With half-pay of 6 livres according to a decision of April 4, 1764, sent to the Bureau des Invalides April 5, 1764.

BATON, JEAN CRISTOPHE
Died at Natchitoches May 31, 1755, Hazeur's company.

BATTELIER, FRANCOIS

BATTELIER, FRANCOIS
With half-pay of 6 livres per month, according to a decision of April 4, 1764, sent to the Bureau des Invalides April 5, 1764.

BATTIN, FRANCOIS
Discharged September 15, 1763, roll of January 1, 1763, folio 23.

BAUBY, CLAUDE CYPRIEN
With half-pay of 15 livres per month, according to a decision of April 4, 1764, sent to the Bureau des Invalides April 5, 1764.

BAUDEMONT, LOUIS
Discharged March 1, 1751.

BAUDEMONT, PIERRE
Died. Company of Le Verrier. The date of his death is not on the roll

BAUDEREL, JACQUES LAURENT
Discharged June 1, 1751.

BAUDET, YVES
Invalid. Went to France on the Samson October 1, 1769, roll of January 1, 1763, folio 37.

BAUDET, YVES

BAUDIN, ANTOINE ROBERT
Discharged September 15, 1763, roll of January 1, 1763, folio 6.

BAUDIN, MATHIEU DENIS

BAUDIN, PIERRE JOSEPH
Died October 4, 1751.

BAUDOUIN, CHARLES
Discharged October 16, 1751.

BAUDOUIN, HEAB
Died at the hospital January 6, 1756, Neyon's company.

BAUDOIN, NICOLAS
With half-pay of 4 livres, 10 sols per month according to a decision of April 4, 1764, sent to the Bureau des Invalides April 5, 1764. Discharged September 15, 1763.

BAUDOUX, JEAN
With half-pay of 6 livres per month according to a decision of April 4, 1764, sent to the Bureau des Invalides April 5, 1764. Discharged September 15, 1763.

BAUDRON, FRANCOIS SIMON
Discharged February 6, 1770, Duplessis' company.

BAUDRY, PIERRE (called) BELLEROSE
Died March 8, 1744, Macarty's company.

BAUDYER, YVES

BAULE, ANTOINE
Discharged September 15, 1763, roll of January 1, 1763, folio 1.

BAUVAIS, CLAUDE CIPRIEN
Discharged September 15, 1763, roll of January 1, 1763, folio 19.

BRAVET or BAVRET, CLAUDE FRANCOIS
Died in Illinois February 28, 1763, roll of January 1, 1763, folio 22.

BAZILLE, JOSEPH FRANCOIS
Broken (on the wheel?) (rompu vif) for having assassinated his (superior) officer and executed June 7, 1757, Trant's company. On the roll of June 1, 1760 he is listed as Joseph Francois Barille.

BEAT JEAN

BEAU, ETIENNE
Discharged September 15, 1763, roll of January 1, 1763, folio 13.

BEAUCHESNE, LAURENT
Discharged August 20, 1770.

BEAUCHESEN, LAURENT
Discharged February 1, 1768, roll of January 1, 1763, folio 36.

BEAUDEOIN, FRANCOIS
Deserted July 4, 1755.

BEAUDET, FRANCOIS
Discharged September 1763, roll of January 1, 1763, folio 4.

BEAUDRAP, PHILIBERT
Died in November, 1755, Varennes' company.

BEAUFIN, HENRY
Discharged September 15, 1763, roll of January 1, 1763, folio 19.

BEAUGRAND, JEAN
Deserted June 15, 1756.

BEAUREGARD, JEAN
Drummer. With half-pay of 6 livres per month according to a decision of April 4, 1764, sent to the Bureau des Invalides April 5, 1764.

BEAULIEU, ETIENNE
Drowned in the sinking of the Pere de Famille February 17, 1770, returning to France.

BEAUVAIS, AUBIN

BEAUVERLET, LAMBERT

BEAUVRI (?), ANTOINE
Discharged February 6, 1770, Mazilliere's company.

BEC, CLEMENT

BEDACRES (or) BEDAGUES, JEAN
Discharged September 15, 1763, roll of January 1, 1763, folio 6.

BEDAQUE, JEAN
With half-pay of 9 livres per month according to a decision of April 4, 1764, sent to the Bureau des Invalides April 5, 1764. Arrived at Bordeaux February 22, 1770. Sergeant.

BEDOUET, FRANCOIS
Died at the hospital September 16, 1769, roll of January 1, 1763, folio 48.

BEIGNOT, PIERRE
Deserted October 20, 1757.

BELETTE, ANSELME

BELIN, JOSEPH ALEXIS

BELLARD, LOUIS LUCIEN
Died December 27, 1767. Roll of January 1, 1763, folio 35.

BELLEGARDE, JEAN BAPTISTE
Discharged April 18, 1756; went to France.

BELLUQUE, CLAUDE
Discharged May 1, 1750.

BENARD, ETIENNE LOUIS
Discharged April 11, 1756, d'Organ's company.

BENAYE, ANDRÉ
Deserted at the Balize November 10, 1745, Le Verrier's company.

BENETOT, CLAUDE
Died November 9, 1751.

BENOUS, PROSPER
Died June 30, 1738. Certificate at the bureau.

BERANGER, JEAN
Corporal. Discharged February 6, 1770, with half-pay of 9 livres per month according to a decision of April 28, 1770.

BERARD, ANTOINE
Discharged February 6, 1770, Mazilliere's company.

BERARD, ANTOINE
Discharged February 1, 1769, roll of January 1, 1763, folio 37.

BERCEAU, CLAUDE
Discharged August 18, 1751.

BERCAU, MICHEL
Died March 16, 1751.

BERCLE, ADAM
Deserted July 4, 1755.

BERÉ, PIERRE
Died at New Orleans November 10, 1757, Cahvoye's company.

BERÉ, PIERRE
Died at New Orleans November 10, 1757, Chavoye's company.

BERGER, JEAN

BERGER, JEAN BAPTISTE
Discharged. See the roll of Calais of May 2, 1763.

BERGEROT, GUILLAUME
Discharged April 1, 1750.

BERGEROT, JEAN LAURENT
Captain. Discharged September 15, 1763. Roll of January 1, 1763, folio 8.

LOUISIANA TROOPS —:— 1720-1770

BERGEROT, LAURENT
Sergeant with thirty years of service. With half-pay of 12 livres per month, according to a decision of October 25, 1769, sent to the Bureau des Invalides October 27, 1769.

BERNARD, GUILLAUME
Died in France at the hospital of LaRochelle March 27, 1770. The death certificate attached to M. Le Moyne's letter was placed in the records of Isle of Ré for the month of July 1770. Discharged November 30, 1769.

BERNARD, JACQUES
Drowned in the sinking of the Pere de Famille February 17, 1770, returning to France.

BERNARD, JACQUES
Deserted July 17, 1755.

BERNARD, JEAN
Discharged August 20, 1770.

BERNARD, JEAN
Executed by the firing squad February 27, 1751.

BERNARD, JEAN BAPTISTE

BERNARD, JEAN BAPTISTE
Drowned in the sinking of the Pere de Famille February 17, 1770, returning to France.

BERNARD, JEAN BAPTISTE
Drowned at Mobile March 19, 1761. See the roll of the same year, folio 36.

BERNARD, JOSEPH
Died October 26, 1737. Certifictae at the bureau.

BERNARD, LOUIS
Discharged October 8, 1769, roll of January 1, 1763, folio 55.

BERNARDIN, PIERRE

BERRANGER, JEAN

BERRY, ANTOINE
Discharged September 15, 1763, roll of January 1, 1763, folio 24.

BERTHELOT, LOUIS URBAIN
Discharged January 1, 1754.

BERTIN, PIERRE

BERTRANCHE, ETIENNE
Died October 28, 1751.

BERTRAND, CLAUDE
Sergeant. Died October 29, 1756, Benoist's company.

BERTRAND, JEAN

BERTRAND, JEAN
Died at the hospital December 25, 1754, Pontalba's company.

BERTRAND, MATHIEU
Stayed in Arcankas (sic) since December 31, 1769, roll of January 1, 1763, folio 51.

BERTRAND, MAXIMILIEN

BERTRAND, NICOLAS
Died at the hospital November 1, 1756, la Tour's company.

BESANCON, PIERRE JOSEPH
Discharged September 15, 1763, roll of January 1, 1763, folio 2.

BESCHET, JEAN

BESSAND, JACQUES
Died Setember 21, 1734. Certificate at the bureau.

BESSÉ, PIERRE

BESSÉ, PIERRE
Went to France on the Samson October 1, 1769, roll of January 1, 1763, folio 49.

BESSÉ, PIERRE
Discharged February 6, 1770. Villiers' company.

BESSÉ, PIERRE
Discharged September 15, 1763, roll of January 1, 1763, folio 20.

BESSIERE, JEAN

BESSON, VINCENT
Discharged May 15, 1751.

BEZIERES, CLAUDE
Died at English Turn (détour á L'anglois) January 13, 1757, Daubry's company.

BIBO, JEAN BAPTISTE
Deserted August 1, 1758. See the roll of June 1, 1760, folio 6.

BIDALLIER, JOSEPH
With half-pay of 6 livres per month according to a decision of February 25, 1769, sent to the Bureau des Invalides October 17, 1769.

BIDAUX, JEAN BAPTISTE
  Discharged May 1, 1750.
BIDEAUX, ANTOINE
  Discharged May 1, 1751.
BIDEAU, JULIEN FRANCOIS
BIDEAU, PIERRE
BIDOT, FRANCOIS
  Died October 25, 1737. Certificate at the bureau.
BIENFAIT, JEAN BAPTISTE
  Died December 20, 1745, Benoist's comany.
BIGARNE, JACQUES
  Discharged April 18, 1756; went to France.
BIGNER, JOSEPH
BIGOIS, JEAN
BILLARD, JACQUES
  Died at the hospital March 12, 1758. See the roll of June 1, 1760, folio 6.
BILLAUD, JACQUES
BILLAUD, JACQUES
  Discharged February 6, 1770, Mazilliere's company.
BILLET, PIERRE
  Executed by firing squad August 1, 1754, Villemont's company.
BILLOCHON, JEAN
  Died at the hospital July 15, 1755, de la Houssaye's company.
BILLY, MATHIAS
  With half-pay of 6 livres per month according to a decision of April 4, 1764, sent to the Bureau des Invalides April 5, 1764.
BINCHE (or) BINS, MARTIN
  Discharged November 30, 1769.
BION, JOSEPH
  Died November 1, 1750.
BIORIN, JACQUES
  Corporal. Discharged September 15, 1763. Roll of January 1, 1763, folio 6. Half-pay of 9 livres according to a decision of April 4, 1764, sent to the Bureau des Invalides April 5, 1764.
BISQUET, JEAN MARIE
  Discharged April 18, 1756; went to France.

BLAISE, JEAN BAPTISTE
  Discharged March 1, 1756.
BLAIZE, PIERRE
  Discharged September 30, 1769, roll of January 1, 1763, folio 49.
BLANC, ANTOINE
  Deserted July 17, 1755.
BLANC, JEAN
  Died at Fort Chartres October 4, 1757, Monchervaux's company.
BLANCHARD, GABRIEL
BLANCHARD, GABRIEL
  Corporal. Discharged February 6, 1770, with half-pay of 6 livres per month according to a decision of April 28, 1770.
BLANCHARD, GUY
  Habitant since January 11, 1752, Artaud's company.
BLANCHARD, JACQUES
  Went to France on the Samson October 1, 1769.
BLANCHARD, JEAN
  Deserted June 8, 1755.
BLANCHÉ, PIERRE
  Deserted July 1, 1750.
BLANCHET, ANTOINE
  Died at New Orleans October 15, 1757, Grandchamp's company.
BLANCLOEIL, CLEMENT
BLARE, FRANCOIS
  Died in Akancas October 19, 1756, Reggio's company.
BLAZEAU, ALEXANDRE
  Deserted April 9, 1754.
BLEMURE, LOUIS
  Died December 8, 1737. Certificate at the bureau.
BLIN, FRANCOIS
  Discharged October 1, 1750.
BLIN, JEAN
  Died July 22, 1751.
BLIN, LOUIS
  Drowned February 27, 1764, roll of January 1, 1763, folio 27.
BODICHON, NICOLAS
  Died June 3, 1742. Certificate at the bureau.
BODIN, ANTOINE
BODION, HUDINET

LOUISIANA TROOPS —:— 1720-1770

BOËTTE, NICOLAS

BOIDET, PIERRE
Drowned June 24, 1750.

BOILEAU, NICOLAS JOSEPH

BOISDOR(É), LOUIS
Sergeant. Killed by the Indians August 1, 1754, Dorgon's company.

BOISQUET, CHARLES
Died September 28, 1755, d'Orgon's company.

BOIRET, SEBASTIEN
Discharged. See the (roll of Calais of May 2, 1763.)

BOISROGER, JEAN BAPTISTE
Drowned in the sinking of the Pere de Famille February 17, 1770, returning to France, Sergeant.

BOISSINOT, FRANCOIS
Half-pay of 9 livres per month according to a decision of June 11, 1764, sent to the Bureau des Invalides June 12, 1764. Discharged September 15, 1763, folio 9.

BOISSINOT, LOUIS
Discharged September 15, 1763, roll of January 1, 1763, folio 25.

BONAN, CHARLES
Discharged May 1, 1751.

BONDIE, PHILIPPE

BONGAS, JEAN

BONIN, ANTOINE

BONIN, ANTOINE
With half-pay of 9 livres per month according to a decision of June 11, 1764, sent to the Bureau des Invalides June 12, 1764. Discharged September 15, 1763, roll of January 1, 1763, folio 9.

BONNAC, JEAN
Condemned to life imprisonment with hard labor February 9, 1756, Montchervaux's company.

BONNARD, JEAN CLEMENT
Drummer-major in the company of Benoist. Discharged in the colony with half-pay of 10 livres per month October 1, 1766. See the decision of April 15, 1767.

BONNARD, JEAN CLEMENT
Discharged Octber 1, 1766, roll of January 1, 1763, folio 32.

BONNARDEL, FRANCOIS

BONNARME, ETIENNE
Discharged September 30, 1769. Roll of January 1, 1763, folio 38.

BONNE, MICHEL
Discharged August 1, 1750.

BONNEAU, JACQUES
Died at the hospital March 21, 1757, Gourdon's company.

BONNEAU, JACQUES
Died at the hospital March 21, 1757. See the roll of June 1, 1760, folio 8.

BONNEAU, JEAN PIERRE

BONNEFOY, ISAAC
Drowned in the river July 9, 1757, Desmazellieres' company.

BONNEFOND, JEAN
With half-pay of 6 livres per month according to a decision of April 4, 1764, sent to the Bureau des Invalides April 5, 1764. Discharged November 15, 1763.

BONNEFOND, JOSEPH
Drowned in the river while going to Pointe Coupee March 4, 1764, Pontalba's Company.

BONNEFOND, LEONARD
Died October 28, 1751.

BONNEFOY, JEAN
Deserted the latter part of September 1750.

BONTEMS, FRANCOIS
Deserted March 1757 to the Spaniards. See the roll of June 1, 1760, folio 11.

BONTURE, JEAN BAPTISTE
Died at the hospital November 7, 1756, Reggio's company.

LOUISIANA TROOPS —:— 1720-1770

BONVALET, ANTOINE
Died at the Balize January 1, 1755, la Gautraye's company.

BONY, JEAN
Died, company of Grandpre. The date of his death is not on the roll. Sent in 1746.

BORDAT, ANTOINE

BORIN, JEAN BAPTISTE

BORME, JEAN LOUIS
Discharged February 1, 1751.

BORNARME, ETIENNE
Carried (on the roll of) 1752.

BOSQUET, PIERRE
With half-pay of 9 livres per month according to a decision of September 8, 1770.

BOSQUET, PIERRE
With half-pay of 9 livres per month according to a decision of April 4, 1764, sent to the Bureau des Invalides April 5, 1764, payable at Rodez in Rouergne. Discharged September 15, 1763. Corporal.

BOSSET, JEAN
Died November 20, 1737. Certificate at the bureau.

BOU, PIERRE ELIE

BOUCARD, ANDRÉ
Deserted August 10, 1754.

BOUCHERIE, JEAN
Discharged September 15, 1763, roll of Januaary 1, 1763, folio 4.

BOUDARD, LOUIS FRANCOIS
Died in 1746.

BOUDARD, LOUIS FRANCOIS
Died September 3, 1746, de Blanc's company.

BOUDRON, PIERRE
Discharged September 15, 1763, roll of January 1, 1763, folio 1.

BOUGINOT, NICOLAS

BOUILLON, ANDRÉ
Discharged September 15, 1763, roll of January 1, 1763 folio 16.

BOUILLOT PIERRE
Died at the hospital October 1, 1755, Gamont's company.

BOUILLY, VINCENT
Discharged August 27, 1756.

BOULANNE, JEAN

BOULANGER, JEAN
Deserted in April, 1754.

BOULANGER, LOUIS
Discharged September 15, 1763, roll of January 1, 1763, folio 7. With half-pay of 9 livres per month according to a decision of June 11, 1764, sent to the Bureau des Invalides June 12, 1764.

BOULANGER, PIERRE
Discharged February 15, 1763, roll of January 1, 1763 folio, 8.

BOULARD, LAURENT
Discharged September 30, 1769, roll of January 1, 1763, folio 42.

BOULARD, LOUIS
Discharged September 15, 1763, roll of January 1, 1763, folio 8.

BOULÉ, JULIEN
Discharged September 15, 1763, roll of January 1, 1763, folio 22.

BOULET, JEAN
Discharged September 15, 1763. Roll of January 1, 1763, folio 13.

BOULLANGER, FRANCOIS LE
Died June 26, 1736. Certificate at the bureau.

BOUQUET, ANTOINE DAUJA
Discharged September 15, 1763, roll of January 1, 1763, folio 11.

BOUQUET, JACQUES

BOUQUET, JACQUES
Discharged February 6, 1770, with half-pay of 6 livres per month, according to a decision of April 28, 1770.

BOURBON, JEAN
Discharged September 15, 1763, roll of January 1, 1763 folio 19.

LOUISIANA TROOPS —:— 1720-1770

BOURCIER, PIERRE
With half-pay of 6 livres per month according to a decision of May 21, 1765, sent to the Bureau des Invalides May 22, 1765.

BOURCIN, FRANCOIS
Entered service May 1, 1769. Discharged October 8, 1769, roll of January 1, 1763, folio 55.

BOURDEL NICOLAS PAUL
Died at the hospital of New Orleans August 20, 1759. See the roll of June 11, 1761, folio 2.

BOUREE, JEAN FRANCOIS
Died September 26, 1737. Certificate at the bureau.

BOURDELAIS, JEAN LOUIS
Died at the hospital September 13, 1767, roll of January 1, 1763, folio 34.

BOURDET, JEAN

BOURDON, JACQUES

BOURDON, JACQUES
Discharged February 6, 1770, with half-pay of 6 livres per month, beginning with the day of his discharge, according to a decision of August 21, 1770. Vaugine's company.

BOURGEOIS, ANDRÉ
Discharged May 1, 1751. Habitant.

BOURGEOIS, FRANCOIS
Soldier. With half-pay of 6 livres per month according to a decision of March 12, 1764, sent to the Bureau des Invalides the same day.

BOURGEOIS, JEAN GABRIEL

BOURGEOIS, JEAN GABRIEL
Discharged February 6, 1770, with half-pay of 4 livres 10 sols per month, according to a decision of April 21, 1770.

BOURGEOIS, PAUL MAURICE (?)
With half-pay of 6 livres per month, according to a decision of April 4, 1764, sent to the Bureau des Invalides April 5, 1764.

BOURGEOIS, PIERRE
Drowned October 22, 1738, in Illinois convoy.

BOURGEONNEAU, JEAN
With half-pay of 6 livres per month according to a decision of April 4, 1764, sent to the Bureau des Invalides April 5, 1764.

BOURGUIGNON, JOSEPH
Discharged October 31, 1769, roll of January 1, 1763, folio 36.

BOURIER, NICOLAS
Discharged September 15, 1763, roll of January 1, 1763, folio 9.

BOURILIAC, JEAN
Executed by the firing squad May 6, 1751.

BOURSIN, FRANCOIS
Discharged September 1, 1764, roll of January 1, 1763, folio 30.

BOUTÉ, CLAUDE
Discharged May 1, 1750.

BOUTEILLE, JEROME
Discharged September 15, 1763, roll of January 1, 1763, folio 7.

BOUTEILLE, JEROME
Drummer.

BOUTROU, PIERRE
Sergeant. With half-pay of 20 livres per month according to a decision of April 4, 1764, sent to the Bureau des Invalides April 5, 1764.

BOUTTÉ, JEAN
Disbanded (licencié) at Havre. See the general roll of February 22, 1761, folio 7. Sent from this port (by) order of the King dated July 10, 1761, to petition for his discharge (papers) which were stolen from him in Paris on Madelaine Street.

BOUTESELLE, CHARLES
Discharged October 8, 1769, roll of January 1, 1763, folio 43.

BOUTTESELLE, CHARLES
Drummer. Drowned in the sinking of the Pere de Famille February 17, 1770, returning to France.

BOUTON, MATHIEU DENIS
Executed by firing squad April 15, 1763. Roll of January 1, 1763, folio 10.

BOUTON, NICOLAS
Died in Illinois February 23, 1755, Reggio's company.

BOUTONNET, NICOLAS
Died November 30, 1751.

BOUTY, PIERRE ANTOINE SIMON
With half-pay of 6 livres per month according to a decision of March 12, 1764, sent to the Bureau des Invalides the same day. Discharged July 1, 1764.

BOUVILLE, MASSON
Died October 4, 1754, D'Erneville's company Cadet á l'Eguillette.

BOUVRY, FRANCOIS
Went to France on the Cameleon October 1, 1764.

BOYAUX, PIERRE
With half-pay of 6 livres per month.

BOYAUX, PIERRE
Native of Lyon. Served seventeen years. Discharged in Louisiana November 30, 1768. Presented his discharge (papers) to the Bureau (and) obtained half-pay of 6 livres per month, according to a decision of June 18, 1769, sent to the Bureau des Invalides.

BOYER, CHARLES
Deserted April 1 1754. Returned.

BOYER, CHARLES

BRAGANCE, FELICAN ALBERT
Discharged September 15, 1763, roll of January 1, 1763, folio 20.

BRAGNARD, NICOLAS
Discharged November 30, 1769, roll of January 1, 1763, folio 47.

BRAILLARD, ANTOINE
Extended leave discharge and went to France on the royal flute Fortune January 1, 1759. See the roll of June 1, 1760, folio f

BRANDE, DOMINQUE
Executed by the firing squad July 14, 1745, for sedition. Gauvrit's company.

BRANGÉ, ETIENNE
Died October 18, 1750.

BRAZIER, PIERRE
Died "Ie der (last day?)" of June, 1751.

BREDAT, ANTOINE

BREMONTIER, PIERRE
Died at Mobile December 6, 1759. See the roll of June 1, 1760, folio 11.

BRETTE, SEBASTIAN
Died October 3, 1736. Certificate at the bureau.

BRETTON, MICHEL
Died at the hospital November 19, 1754, De Bonnille's company.

BRIDEL, JACQUES
Died December 20, 1751.

BRIDEL, PIERRE

LOUISIANA TROOPS —:— 1720-1770

BRIE, CHEVALIER DE
Cadet a l'aiguillette. Died at Fort Chartres December 26, 1756, Traut's company.

BRIGNAC, JACQUES

BRIGNAC, JACQUES SIMON
Died at Alibamons ("aux Alibamons") August 10, 1754, Gourdon's company.

BRIGNAC, MATHIEU or JACQUES
With half-pay of 4 livres 10 sols per month according to a decision of June 11, 1764, sent to the Bureau des Invalides June 12, 1764. Discharged September 15, 1763, roll of January 1, 1763, folio 10.

BRIGNAC, MICHEL
Discharged September 15, 1763, roll of January 1, 1763, folio 23.

BRIGNAC, PIERRE SIMON
With half-pay of 4 livres 10 sols per month according to a decision of June 11, 1764, sent to the Bureau des Invalides June 12, 1764. Discharged September 15, 1763, roll of January 1, 1763, folio 11.

BRION, RENÉ

BRISSET, GABRIEL

BRISSET, SIMON

BROC, ANTOINE
Died August 28, 1751.

BROCHE, JEAN
Died August 29, 1751.

BROLLIARD, SIMON

BROSSEAU, JEAN BAPTISTE
Deserted August 30, 1761. See the roll of the same year, folio 16.

BROUET, PIERRE

BROUILLARD, JEAN BAPTISTE
Discharged August 1, 1750.

BROUILLARD, JEAN BAPTISTE
Discharged August 1, 1750.

BROUILLARD, NICOLAS
Discharged November 30, 1769, roll of January 1, 1763, folio 48.

BROUTIN, NARCIS

BROYARD, ETIENNE
Habitant since January 13, 1753.

BROUYARD, SIMON
Discharged August 20, 1770, with half-pay of 6 livres per month, according to a decision of October 17, 1770.

BRULÉ, BARTHELEMY
Died at the hospital August 10, 1756, Desmazellieres' company.

BRUNEAU, JOSEPH
Discharged May 1, 1751.

BRUNEAU, LOUIS PIERRE

BRUNEAU, MARIN

BRUNET, JACQUES

BRUNET, JOSEPH
Deserted June 15, 1756.

BRUNET, PIERRE

BRUNO, JEAN
Died at the hospital October 29, 1754, Villemont's company.

BRUNOT, JEAN AUGUSTIN
Discharged September 15, 1763, roll of January 1, 1763, folio 12.

BRUNOT, PIERRE

BRUXELLES, ETIENNE
Went to France on the ship Orphée March 17, 1769, roll of January 1, 1763, folio 41.

BUFETAUD, JOACHIM
Discharged July 10, 1756; went to France.

BUISSON, LOUIS

BUISSON, LOUIS
Discharged February 6, 1770, Vaugine's company.

BUNEL, JACQUES
Discharged November 30, 1769, roll of January 1, 1763, folio 42.

BURAUX, JEAN
Discharged April 1, 1764, roll of January 1, 1763, folio 29.

BUREAU, NOEL PHILIPES
Deserted. Condemned by contumacy to be executed by firing squad. See the procedure of May 15, 1753.

LOUISIANA TROOPS —:— 1720-1770

BUSIGNY, BERNARD
 Drowned at the Balize January 10, 1754, du Tillet's company.

BUTEUX, LOUIS
 Died at Illinois August 1, 1756, Dutillet's company.

BUTOR, FRANCOIS

BUTTEAUX, JEAN
 Discharged August 1, 1750.

BUTTEUX, LOUIS

LOUISIANA TROOPS —:— 1720-1770

CABANNES, MARTIN
Died November 6, 1761. See the roll of the same year, folio 17.

CABAT, NICOLAS

CADET, LEONARD
Discharged September 30, 1769, roll of January 1, 1763, folio 42.

CADRON, JEAN
Demoted and condemned to the gallies for life.

CAF, FRANCOIS
Deserted February 1, 1759, see the roll of June 1, 1760, folio 12.

CAFFIN, PAUL
Died, Marest's company. The date of his death is not on the roll.

CAILLÉ, JEAN
Discharged May 1, 1751.

CAILLÉ, JOSEPH
Discharged June 1, 1751.

CAILLAUX, FRANCOIS
Sergeant. Deserted August 30, 1761. See the roll of that year, folio 23.

CAILLEAUX or CAILLEUX, JEAN
Deserted June 3, 1757, company of Montberault. See the roll of June 1, 1760, folio 6, where he is carried under the name of Cailleux.

CAILLOU, ETIENNE
Discharged December 30, 1763, according to the cartouche deposited in the carton labeled Cartouche No. 137. He has served since 1752, company of Villiers.

CAILLET, PIERRE

CAILLET, PIERRE
Discharged February 6, 1770, with half-pay of 6 livres per month according to a decision of October 17, 1770.

CAILLEUX, NICOLAS
Discharged April 1, 1756.

CAJOT, PIERRE
Discharged November 1, 1751.

CALANDREAU, CLAUDE FRANCOIS
Discharged September 15, 1763, roll of January 1, 1763, folio 16.

CALASSON, FRANCOIS

CALASSON, FRANCOIS
Drowned in the sinking of the Pere de Famille February 17, 1770, returning to France.

CALBARENS, JEAN
Discharged September 15, 1763, roll of January 1, 1763, folio 12.

CALMES, ETIENNE
With half-pay of 6 livres per month, according to a decision of December 10, 1765, sent to the Bureau des Invalides, April 13, 1765. Discharged September 1, 1764.

CALVÉ, JULIEN

CAMUS, JEAN
Discharged September 30, 1769, roll of January 1, 1763, folio 48.

CANELLE, SIEUR
Cadet a l'aiguillette.
Died August 18, 1746.

CANTEL, PIERRE
Discharged September 15, 1763, roll of January 1, 1763, folio 5.

CAPRON, FRANCOIS

CARABÉ, DOMINIQUE
Discharged May 1, 1751.

CARDEUR, CLAUDE

CARDEUR, CLAUDE
Drummer. Discharged February 6, 1770, with half-pay of 6 livres per month counting from July 1, 1770, according to a decision of October 1, 1769, company of Trudeau.

CARDEUR, CLAUDE
Discharged February 6, 1770, carried with half-pay of 6 livres per month.

CARDINAL or CHARDINEL, JEAN BAPTISTE

CARE, DOMINIQUE
Deserted June 15, 1756.

LOUISIANA TROOPS — :— 1720-1770

CARELARD, MICHEL
Deserted September 1, 1754.

CARLIER, JEAN PIERRE

CARLIER, JEAN PIERRE
Discharged September 15, 1763, roll of January 1, 1763, folio 24.

CARLIN, DOMINIQUE

CARLIN, JOSEPH
Discharged October 8, 1769, roll of January 1, 1763, folio 47.

CARNIER, LAURENT
Discharged September 15, 1763, roll of January 1, 1763, folio 25.

CARON, FRANCOIS

CARPINET, HONORÉ
Died November 7, 1750.

CARRÉ, CHARLES

CARRÉ, ETIENNE

CARRÉ, FRANCOIS
Discharged September 30, 1769, roll of January 1, 1763, folio 48.

CARRON, FRANCOIS
Drowned in Bayou St. Jean February 10, 1766, roll of January 1, 1763, folio 32.

CARTOIR or CATOIR, ANTOINE

CASADE, LOUIS

CASBERGUE, MATH.

CASBERGUE, MATHURIN
Discharged September 15, 1763, roll of January 1, 1763, folio 25.

CASMANN, MARC
Went to France on the Samson October 1, 1769, roll of January 1, 1763, folio 51.

CASSADE, LOUIS
Discharged February 6, 1770, with half-pay of 4 livres 10 sols per month according to a decision of April 28, 1770.

CASSAIGNE, JOSEPH
Discharged September 1, 1761. See the roll of the same year, folio 27.

CASSOU, ANTOINE
Discharged August 10, 1754.

CASTAGNET, LAURENT
Deserted June 3, 1757 at Fort Chartres. See the roll of June 1, 1760, folio 11.

CASTEL, ALAIN
Drowned in the sinking of the Pere de Famille February 17, 1770, returning to France.

CASTELIN, PIERRE

CASTELAIN, PIERRE

CASTILLE, SALVADOR
Drowned in the river, descending from Natchez October 2, 1754, company of Pontalba.

CAUMET, MATHIEU
Drowned in the river, Hazeur's company. The roll of December 24, 1758, makes no mention of the year in which he was drowned.

CAUNOIR, PIERRE

CAUNOIR, PIERRE
Sergeant. Discharged February 6, 1770, with half-pay of 12 livres per month according to a decision of April 28, 1770.

CAUSSIN, JEAN BAPTISTE MARC

CAUVIN, ANTOINE
Discharged July 1, 1765, roll of January 1, 1763, folio 32.

CAUX, RAYMOND
With half-pay of 6 livres per month, according to a decision of April 4, 1764, sent to the Bureau des Invalides April 5, 1764.

CAVALIER, CLAUDE
Sergeant. With half-pay of 12 livres per month according to a decision of June 11, 1764, sent the same day to the Bureau des Invalides.

CAVALLIER, ANDRÉ
Discharged September 15, 1763, roll of January 1, 1763, folio 18.

CAVALLIER, JEAN
Discharged July 10, 1756 and went to France on the Rhinoceros.

CAVARS, CLAUDE

LOUISIANA TROOPS —:— 1720-1770

CAVIER, NICOLAS
With half-pay of 9 livres per month payable at Amiens, according to a decision of September 8, 1770, sent to the Bureau des Invalides September 14, 1770, "de la Reforme de September 15, 1763."

CELENIX, FRANCOIS
Deserted January 29, 1763, roll of January 1, 1763, folio 24.

CENANT, LOUIS
Soldier. With half-pay of 9 livres per month according to a decision of April 4, 1764, sent to the Bureau des Invalides April 5, 1764. Discharged September 15, 1763.

CERAIZE, JOSEPH

CERINGE, NICOLAS
Discharged May 1, 1750.

CERIZIER, MICHEL
Discharged July 10, 1756, went to France

CERTAIN, FRANCOIS

CERVRAIZE, CLAUDE

CERVRAIZE, CLAUDE

CHABEAU, JEAN CHARLES FRANCOIS
Deserted March 4, 1754.

CHABERT, JOSEPH
Died at Illinois November 22, 1754, company of de la Houssaye.

CHALIN, MICHEL
Died in Argansas June 22, 1766, roll of January 1, 1763, folio 33.

CHALOCHE, ANTOINE
With half-pay of 6 livres per month, according to a decision of April 4, 1764, sent to the Bureau des Invalides April 5, 1764. Discharged September 15, 1763, roll of January 1, 1763, folio 7.

CHAMBON, ESTIENNE
Discharged May 1, 1765, roll of January 1, 1763, folio 33.

CHAMBON, JEAN
Discharged September 15, 1756.

CHAMBRIE, FRANCOIS
Discharged July 1, 1764, roll of January 1, 1763, folio 29.

CHAMBRIE, FRANCOIS
Died October 10, 1751.

CHAMPAGNE, JEAN BAPTISTE

CHAMPAGNE, JEAN
Died September 30, 1750.

CHAMPRE, JEAN
Died August 19, 1735. Death certificate at the bureau in proper form.

CHANGEUX, ETIENNE
Died at the hospital June 21, 1756, Chavois' company.

CHANTRE, PIERRE
Died October 26, 1751.

CHAPART, ARNOULT
Discharged June 1, 1750.

CHAPELIN

CHAPELLE, JEAN
Died October 27, 1751.

CHAPERON, ETIENNE
Sergeant. Discharged September 15, 1763. With half-pay of 15 livres per month according to a decision of April 4, 1764, sent to the Bureau des Invalides April 5, 1764.

CHAPSAL, ANTOINE

CHAPUY, FRANCOIS
Discharged March 9, 1764, roll of January 1, 1763, folio 27.

CHARDON, JACQUES

CHAREMBEAU, JEAN
Discharged November 15, 1769, roll of January 1, 1763, folio 50.

CHAREMBERG, GUILLAUME
Discharged October 30, 1769, roll of January 1, 1763, folio 52.

CHARMIER, JEAN FRANCOIS

CHAREY, MICHEL

CHARLIER, REMY

CHARLIER, REMY
Discharged February 6, 1770, with half-pay of 4 livres 10 sols per month, according to a decision of April 28, 1770.

CHARPENTIER, JOSEPH
Died at the hospital December 30, 1757, company of Desvarennes.

CHARPENTIER, MICHEL DENIS

CHARPENTIER, MICHEL DENIS
Discharged February 6, 1770, company of Trudeau.

CHARPENTIER, PIERRE
Discharged July 5, 1756.

CHARROYE, CLAUDE
Deserted March 29, 1758, and condemned by contumacy to be hung, by judgment of July 24. See the roll of June 1, 1760, folio 10.

CHARVET, FRANCOIS

CHASSE, ANTOINE
Discharged July 1, 1751.

CHASSEY, MICHEL
Fusileer. Discharged August 20, 1770, with half-pay of 6 livres per month, according to a decision of October 17, 1770.

CHASSOT, JOSEPH

CHATELIN, PIERRE
Stayed at Arcankas December 1, 1769, roll of January 1, 1763, folio 50.

CHATELLIER, FRANCOIS
Discharged September 15, 1763, with half-pay of 4 livres 10 sols per month according to a decision of April 4, 1764, sent to the Bureau des Invalides April 5, 1764.

CHAULET, DAMIEN
Discharged February 6, 1770, company of Villiers.

CHAUMONNEAU, FRANCOIS
Died October 12, 1737. Death certificate at the bureau in proper form.

CHAUOIN, PIERRE
Sergeant. With half-pay of 15 livres per month according to a decision of November 28, 1764, sent to the Bureau des Invalides November 5, 1764.

CHAUSSADE, FRANCOIS

CHAUSSELIGNE, GUILLEAUME
Died at the hospital November 13, 1757, company of Murat. See the roll of June 1, 1760, folio 12, where he is named Chausselegue.

CHAUVES, FRANCOIS FIRMIN
Died November 4, 1756, at the hospital, company of Grandchamp.

CHAUVET, JEAN BAPTISTE

CHAUVET, JEAN BAPTISTE
Discharged February 6, 1770, company of Trudeau.

CHAUVIN, PIERRE
Discharged July 14, 1764, roll of January 1, 1763, folio 35.

CHAUX, PIERRE
Recruited soldier taken upon arrival in Louisiana on the vessel St. Claude in 1756. Debarked at Boulogne May 1, 1763, presented himself to the Bureau the 17th of the same month with passport of the same day, May 1, which was visaed to give him full leave.

CHAVANNE, LOUIS DE

CHELATRE, MICHEL
Habitant. Discharged July 1, 1751.

CHELINGRE, JOSEPH

CHEMIN, GILLES

CHENEL, FRANCOIS

CHENEL, LOUIS JACQUES
Discharged August 10, 1754.

CHENESTRE, FREDERIC
Died September 1, 1751.

CHEREL, ROBERT

CHERLY, PIERRE
Deserted August 1, 1758. See the roll of June 1, 1760, folio 6.

CHERON, PIERRE
Deserted July 11, 1757, at Vera Cruz. See the roll of June 1, 1760, folio 10.

CHERVIEUX, JEAN CLAUDE
Died at the hospital October 9, 1756, company of Grandchamp.

CHESNAU, PHILIPPES FRANCOIS

CHEVAL, MICHEL
CHEVALIER, CHRISTOPHE
CHEVALLIER, CLAUDE
  Executed by firing squad June 16, 1751.
CHEVALIER, JACQUES
  Deserted the last of August, 1750.
CHEVALIER, LOUIS
  With half-pay of 6 livres per month according to a decision of April 4, 1764, sent to the Bureau des Invalides April 5, 1764. Discharged September 15, 1763.
CHEVALIER, NICOLAS
  Died at the hospital September 2, 1767, roll of January 1, 1763, folio 34.
CHEVALIER, PIERRE
CHEVEL or CHENEL, FRANCOIS
  Discharged July 1, 1750.
CHEVERRY, DOMINIQUE
  Died November 7, 1751.
CHEVERT, BENOIT
  Discharged September 30, 1769, roll of January 1, 1763, folio 38.
CHEVERT, GUILLAUME
  Discharged September 15, 1763, roll of January 1, 1763, folio 4.
CHEVEUX, LAURENT
  Died at Mobile, August 27, 1754, company of La Gautraye.
CHEVRETY, LAURENT
  Discharged May 1, 1751.
CHEVREY, SIMON
  Discharged April 1, 1756.
CHIMENNE, ANTOINE
CHIRE, CHARLES
  Executed by firing squad June 3, 1750.
CHIRON, PAUL
  Died in Missouris May 15, 1763, roll of January 1, 1760, folio 11.
CHIRVET, BENOIST
CHOLET, DAMIEN
CHOLTS, IGNACE
  Died August 28, 1738. Death certificatee at the bureau in proper form.

CHOP, JEAN TOBIE
  Deserted July 17, 1755.
CHOP, JOSEPH
  Discharged September 30, 1769, roll of January 10, 1763, folio 46.
CHUISTRE, CHRISOSTOME
  Died September 3, 1751.
CIRQUE, JEAN
  Discharged September 15, 1763, roll of January 1, 1763, folio 20.
CIRIER, JOSEPH
  Discharged June 17, 1751.
CLAIRET, CHARLES
  Discharged September 15, 1763, roll of January 1, 1763, folio 5.
CLAIRET, JEAN
  Discharged September 15, 1763, roll of January 1, 1763, folio 8.
CLAUDON, ANTOINE
  Discharged September 15, 1763, roll of January 1, 1763, folio 25.
CLAVEL, CLAUDE
  Died October 21, 1736. Certificate at the bureau in proper form.
CLAVET, MICHEL GERARD
  Killed or taken (prisoner) by the Cherakis or Chicachas Indians, November 9, 1757, Grandpre's company.
CLEMENT, JEAN JOSEPH
  Died November 15, 1751.
CLIGNOT, JEAN BAPTISTE
  Discharged June 1, 1751.
CLIGNY, NICOLAS
  Deserted February 5, 1739. He was a corporal.
CLONIER, PIERRE JOSEPH
  Deserted February 5, 1739.
CLOQUET, BERNARD
  Discharged September 15, 1763, roll of January 1, 1763, folio 16.
CLOZEAUX, FRANCOIS
COCHARD, GUILLAUME
COCHARD, NICOLAS
  Died October 15, 1751.

COCHET, ETIENNE
With half-pay of 6 livres per month according to a decision of April 4, 1764, sent to the Bureau des Invalides April 5, 1764. Discharged September 15, 1763.

COCHOIS, PIERRE
Discharged May 29, 1754. Went to France.

COCHU, CHARLES LEGER
Layed off at Lavre; see the general roll of February 22, 1761. He was sent from this post with half-pay.

CODAU or CAUDAY, CHARLES
Discharged September 15, 1763, roll of January 1, 1763, folio 6.

COLAIN, JEAN BAPTISTE
Deserted August 30, 1761. See the roll of the same year, 1761, folio 33. He arrived in Louisiana in 1757.

COLASSE, JEAN CLAUDE
Died at the hospital March 30, 1757, company of Neyon.

COLETTE, GILLES

COLETTE, LOUIS
Discharged September 15, 1763, roll of January 1, 1763, folio 7.

COLIN, FRANCOIS
Discharged May 1, 1750.

COLIN, JEAN BAPTISTE

COLIN, JEAN BAPTISTE
Died July 4, 1755, company of Artaud.

COLIN, LOUIS
Discharged September 15, 1763, roll of January 1, 1763, folio 14.

COLIN, NICOLAS
Indefinite leave, went to France on the royal vessel Fortune January 1, 1759. See the roll of June 1, 1761

COLLET, ANDRÉ

COLLET, JEAN BAPTISTE
Died August 15, 1745, Macarthy's company.

COLLMARE, JEAN
Discharged September 15, 1763, roll of January 1, 1763, folio 26.

COLLU, MARIN
Died September 3, 1750.

COLOMB, JOSEPH
Discharged September 15, 1763, roll of January 1, 1763, folio 2.

COLOMB, PHILIPPES

COLOMB, THIERRY JOSEPH

COFINIAQUE, PIERRE
Deserted July 19, 1755, and condemned to the gallies July 29, 1755.

COMBESSEUZE, FRANCOIS
Died October 22, 1750.

COMBLE, PIERRE

COMBLE, PIERRE
Discharged February 6, 1770, company of Duplessis.

COMPARIOUS, JEAN
Discharged September 15, 1763, roll of January 1, 1763, folio 8.

CONDAMIN, JEAN
Discharged April 18, 1756 and went to France on the flute Messager.

CONFENIAC, PIERRE

CONNANT, LOUIS
Discharged March 31, 1761. See the roll of the same year, folio 21. With half-pay of 6 livres per month according to a decision of April 4, 1764, sent to the Bureau des Invalides April 5, 1764.

CONNARD, PIERRE

CONNOIR, PAUL

CONTRESTY, PIERRE

COPIN or COUPIN, JEAN
Died September 3, 1756, Bonnille's company.

COQUELIN, JACQUES

COQUET, JACQUES
Discharged September 15, 1763, roll of January 1, 1763, folio 13.

LOUISIANA TROOPS —:— 1720-1770

COQUIER, JULIEN
Discharged October 31, 1769, roll of January 1, 1763, folio 42.

COQUILLARD, NICOLAS
Remained in Arcankas December 31, 1769, roll of January 1, 1763, folio 50.

CORDIER, BLAISE
Died at the hospital February 17, 1756, company of Populus.

CORDONNIER, ETIENNE

CORDONNIER, JEAN BAPTISTE
Died at the hospital at New Orleans October 9, 1757, company of Grandchamp.

CORNE, GABRIEL
Died November 15, 1764, roll of January 1, 1763, folio 27.

CORONI, FRANCOIS
Died January 28, 1738. Death certificate at the bureau in proper form.

CORSONNET, CHARLES FRANCOIS

CORTESY, LOUIS
Discharged September 15, 1763. With half-pay of 4 livres 10 sols per month according to a decision of April 4, 1764, sent to the Bureau des Invalides April 5, 1764.

COUDHERE, JACQUES

COURCELLE, JEAN
Died October 7, 1737. Death certificate at the bureau in proper form.

COURDEAU, JEAN LOUIS
Discharged October 21, 1759, being unworthy of serving and went to France on the vessel Union "du Cap Sans le meme tems." See the roll of June 1, 1760, folio 3.

COURSIN or COUSSIN, FOURCY
Died at the hospital at New Orleans September 27, 1751. See the roll of the same year, folio 4.

COURT, JOSEPH

COURT, JOSEPH
Died at Mobile December 21, 1754, company of Favrot.

COUSIN, ANTOINE JOSEPH
Arrived in the colony in 1750, discharged June 1, 1751, as well as being carried on indefinite leave.

COUSIN, GUILLAUME JOSEPH
Executed by firing squad April 6, 1757, Villemont's company.

COUSIN, LOUIS

COUSIN, LOUIS
Drowned in the sinking of the Pere de Famille February 17, 1770, returning to France.

COUTANT, FRANCOIS

COUTURIER, JEAN

COUTURIER, JEAN
Died at Fort Chartres March 9, 1756, company of La Gautraye.

COUTTY, JEAN
Discharged November 30, 1769, roll of January 1, 1763, folio 51.

COUVERT, ANTOINE
Died November 5, 1751.

COUVERT, BLAIZE
Discharged June 1, 1765, roll of January 1, 1763, folio 31.

COUVRECHEF, ADRIEN

COUZIN, GUILLAUME JOSEPH
Deserted February 15 (1757) and executed by a firing squad April 6, 1757, company of Villemont.

CRABER, PIERRE
Died November 2, 1751.

CREMONT, JEAN
Deserted July 19, 1755, and condemned by contumacy to be hung.

CREPIN, HONORÉ
Died August 14, 1734. Death certificate at the bureau in proper form.

CRESSON, ETIENNE
Discharged August 10, 1754.

CRESSON, HUBERT FRANCOIS

CRESSON, HUBERT FRANCOIS
Drowned in the sinking of the Pere de Famille February 17, 1770, returning to France.

LOUISIANA TROOPS —:— 1720-1770

CRETÉ, MICHEL JEROSME
Deserted September 29, 1768, roll of January 1, 1763, folio 36.

CROCHET, JEAN
Discharged November 30, 1769, roll of January 1, 1763, folio 43.

CUSSOR, ANTOINE
Discharged September 15, 1763, roll of January 1, 1763, folio 14.

CRISTAL, ANTOINE ANGE AUGUSTE

CROISY, PIERRE
Deserted October 31, 1751.

CUSSOR, ANTOINE
Died at Illinois September 22, 1755, company of Favrot.

DAGUERRE CHARLES FRANCOIS
Died at the hospital September 11, 1758. See the roll of June 1, 1760, folio 2.

DAIX, GILLES

DALMASSE, JEAN
Deserted August 30, 1761. See the roll of the same year, folio 33.

DAMAR, PIERRE
Drowned in the river October 22, 1756, company of Artuad.

DAMIENS, GUILLAUME
Died January 29, 1734.

DANAY, JEAN LOUIS
Discharged April 18, 1756; went to France.

D'ANGOULEME, JEAN LOUIS
Died December 7, 1751.

DANIS, HONORÉ MARTIAL
With his wife, drowned in the sinking of the Pere de Famille February 17, 1770, returning to France.

DANIS, JULLIEN

DANTONIN, NICOLAS
Discharged June 1, 1751.

DANZIN, GASPARD
Drowned in the river May 11, 1757, company of Chavoye.

DAPOGNET, JACQUES
Discharged May 24, 1756, company of Benoist.

DARDY, JEAN BAPTISTE
Engaged in 1762. Discharged October 8, 1769, roll of January 1, 1763, folio 56.

DASSIGNY, JEAN
Died at Kaskakias May 16, 1755, company of Sommes.

DAUMEAN, ALEXIS
Discharged August 10, 1754.

DAUPHIN, FRANCOIS
Discharged September 15, 1763, roll of January 1, 1763, folio 10.

DAUPHIN, HENRY
With half-pay of 4 livres per month according to a decision of April 4, 1764, sent to the Bureau des Invalides April 5, 1764.

DAUTIN, EDMÉ
Soldier of Amelot's company, died at the New Orleans hospital October 26, 1752. His death certificate legalized by M. Foucault and by M. Le Duc de Praslin, sent to M. Camelin attorney for the king at Auxerre, July, 1769. One remains in the carton in Louisiana.

DAUX, CHARLES
Sergeant. Discharged February 6, 1770, with half-pay of 6 livres per month according to a decision of April 28, 1770.

DAUX, CHARLES
Discharged March 31, 1761. See the roll of the same year, folio 4.

DAVID, CLAUDE
With half-pay of 9 livres per month according to a decision of June 11, 1764, sent to the Bureau des Invalides June 12, 1764, discharged September 15, 1763.

DAVID, JOSEPH
Died September 11, 1751.

DAVION, JEAN BAPTISTE
Discharged April 1, 1750.

DEBARBIER, ETIENNE
Died at Illinois September 15, 1754, company of Monchervaux.

DECARLIN, JOSEPH VINCENT

DECOCHIES, GABRIEL
Discharged September 30, 1769, roll of January 1, 1763, folio 45.

DEDUY, CLAUDE NICOLAS
Died April 30, 1755, company of Dorgon.

DEFIN, JEAN
Died at Mobile, August 24, 1754, company of Grandmaison.

DE FOURRIERE, JEAN BAPTISTE
Died August 12, 1751.

DE GOURDON, LOUIS
Entered service April 1, 1769. Discharged November 30, 1769.

DE HAYE, HENRY JOSEPH

DE LA BROSSE, NICOLAS

LOUISIANA TROOPS —:— 1720-1770

DE LA CHAMBRE, RENÉ

DE LAGE, JEAN
Remained at Illinois, roll of January 1, 1763, folio 38.

DE LANGLOISERIE, JACQUES STE. THEREZE
Died September 21, 1737.

DE LAVIGNE, LAURENT
Canoneer engaged April 1, 1765. Went to France on the Pere de Famille October 8, 1769, roll of January 1, 1768, folio 55.

DELAYNE, NICOLAS JEAN BAPTISTE
Discharged March 31, 1761, roll of the same year, folio 18.

DELFIN, JOANNES
With his wife. Corporal. Invalide. Drowned in the sinking of the Pere de Famille February 17, 1770, returning to France.

DELHAYE, HENRY JOSEPH
Corporal. Discharged February 6, 1770, with half-pay of 6 livres per month, according to a decision of April 28, 1770.

DELIOT, FRANCOIS
Died October 25, 1751.

DELMASSE, JEAN
Discharged. See the roll dated from Calais May 2, 1763.

DELONG, JOSEPH

DELPECHE, LOUIS

DELTON, SILVAIN

DELPUX, JEAN
Deserted at the Cap September 20, 1750.

DEMANECHE or DEMANEGE, BLAIZE
Discharged permanently and went to France on the royal vessel Fortune January 1, 1759. See the roll of June 1, 1760, folio 8.

DE MANTE, JACQUES
Sergeant. With half-pay of 15 livres per month, according to a decision of April 4, 1764, sent to the Bureau des Invalides April 5, 1764.

DEMANTE, NICOLAS MARIN

DEMANY, CAZARD
Deserted June 8, 1755.

DEMAY, LEGER
Sergeant. With half-pay of 15 livres per month according to a decision of April 4, 1764, sent to the Bureau des Invalides April 5, 1764. Discharged September 15, 1768.

DEMOLY, CLAUDE

DE MANTE, NICOLAS MARIN
Corporal. With half-pay of 9 livres per month according to a decision of April 4, 1764, sent to the Bureau des Invalides April 5, 1764. Discharged September 15, 1763.

DENIS, ETIENNE

DENIZMENDY, ALEXANDRE
Discharged August 7, 1751.

DE RETS, CHARLES

DESAIGLES, JEAN
Discharged September 15, 1763, roll of January 1, 1763, folio 10.

DESCHAMPS, CHARLES

DESCHAMPS, JEAN BAPTISTE
With half-pay of 8 livres per month according to a decision of April 4, 1764, sent to the Bureau des Invalides April 5, 1764. Corporal.

DESCLARDINS, LOUIS BENOIT
Drowned in the river February 12, 1754, company of Desmazellieres.

DESCOM, CHARLES
Discharged June 14, 1756. Went to France.

DESCRIMES, GUILLEAUME
Discharged October 8, 1769, roll of January 1, 1763, folio 53.

DE SELLE, JEAN

DESELLE, JEAN
Discharged June 1, 1764, roll of January 1, 1763, folio 26.

DESGAIT, ETIENNE
Parisien. With half-pay of 9 livres per month according to a decision of November 30, 1764, sent to the Bureau des Invalides December 1, 1764.

LOUISIANA TROOPS —:— 1720-1770

DESGOULETS, JEAN
Deserted at Arkancas October 26, 1759. See the roll of June 1, 1760, folio 4.

DES GOUTTES, JEAN

DESJARDINS, FRANCOIS
Discharged September 15, 1763, roll of January 1, 1763, folio 10.

DESMAISONS, SYLVAIN

DESMALLE, JEAN
Died at La Balize April 20, 1765, roll of January 1, 1763, folio 30.

DESMONTS, LOUIS

DESMORTIERS, PIERRE
With half-pay of 6 livres per month according to a decision of April 4, 1764, sent to the Bureau des Invalides April 5, 1764.

DESMOULINS, CHARLES
Died suddenly at New Orleans March 28, 1766, roll of January 1, 1763, folio 33.

DESMOULINS, LOUIS
Died at the hospital May 4, 1756, company of Desmazellieres.

DESMOULINS, NICOLAS

DESNANT, JACQUES

DESNANT, JACQUES
Discharged September 15, 1763, roll of January 1, 1763, folio 25.

DESORMEAUX, JEAN BAPTISTE
Invalid. Discharged.

DESPORTES, LOUIS
Discharged December 31, 1764, roll of January 1, 1763, folio 27.

DESPREZ, ANTOINE
Deserted August 1, 1758. See the roll of June 1, 1759, folio 9.

DESROCHES, ANTOINE
Discharged September 15, 1763, roll of January 1, 1763, folio 24.

DESROZIERS, JACQUES

DESSOUARD, JEAN

DESTOUR, Le Sieur
Merchant from Lyon. Drowned in the sinking of the Pere de Famille February 17, 1770, returning to France.

DESTRÉ, NICOLAS
Roll of January 1, 1763, folio 45.

DESTREVAL, FRANCOIS
Discharged March 1, 1756, company of La Tour.

DESTURBÉ, JACQUES
Condemned to the gallies for life February 9, 1756, company of Artuad.

DESZAIZE or DESRAIZE, JEAN

DETRON, SILVAIN
Discharged September 30, 1769, roll of January 1, 1763, folio 37.

DETROYS, JOSEPH
Discharged September 1, 1761. See the roll of the same year, folio 40. With half-pay of 6 livres per month according to a decision of April 4, 1764, sent to the Bureau des Invalides April 5, 1764.

DEVERS, JEAN
Discharged September 15, 1763, roll of January 1, 1763, folio 15.

DEVIN, MARIN

DEVOST, CLAUDE
Demoted July 2, 1750.

DEVREIGNE, LOUIS
Died at the hospital March 11, 1758. See the roll of June 1, 1760, folio 9.

DEZERT or DESSERT, GUY
Discharged June 1, 1765, roll of January 1, 1763, folio 31.

D'HOMER, JEROSME

DIARD, NICOLAS

DIDIER, CLAUDE PETIT

DIEBEAU or DUBEAU, CLAUDE AUGUSTIN

DIGOIX, JEAN NICOLAS ROMAIN
Discharged June 1, 1751.

DIOT, THOMAS
Discharged August 20, 1770.

DLENÉ, NICOLAS

LOUISIANA TROOPS —:— 1720-1770

DODANE, CLAUDE
Died November 4, 1751.
DODÉ, FRANCOIS
DONIOT, ALEXIS
DONJON, JEAN BAPTISTE
Died at the hospital August 10, 1756, company of Chavoye.
DONNANT, NICOLAS
Drowned in the sinking of the Pere de Famille, February 17, 1770, returning to France.
DORÉ, ANTOINE
Condemned to the gallies July 24, 1755, company of Hazeur.
DORÉ, PIERRE
DOREL, MICHEL
Dscharged July 1, 1765, roll of January 1, 1763.
DORIOT or DAURIAT JEAN FRANCOIS
Died at the hospital June 20, 1759. See the roll of June 1, 1760, folio 6.
DOUCET, FRANCOIS
Discharged September 15, 1763, roll or January 1, 1763, folio 21.
DOUCET, PIERRE
Discharged September 15, 1763, roll of January 1, 1763, folio 4.
DOUCET SIMON PIERRE
Discharged September 15, 1763, roll of January 1, 1763, folio 18.
DOUCHY, HUBERT JEAN
Discharged November 30, 1769, roll of January 1, 1763, folio 41.
DOUSSIN, LOUIS
Died May 2, 1758. See the roll of June 1, 1760, folio 11.
DOUSSIN, MAURICE
DOYEN, LOUIS
DOYEN, LOUIS
Discharged February 6, 1770, with half-pay of 4 livres 10 sols per month according to a decision of April 21, 1770.
DRIEN, PHILIPPE
Discharged May 1, 1755.
DROUART, DENIS
Discharged September 10, 1756.

DRUET, JOSEPH
Died July 11, 1751.
DRUGMAN, JEAN BAPTISTE
With half-pay of 5 livres per month according to a decision of April 4, 1764, sent to the bureau des Invalides April 5, 1764. Sergeant. Discharged September 15, 1763, roll of January 1, 1763, folio 81.
DROMAS, JOSEPH
Drowned in the river March 5, 1754, company of Gamont.
DUAT, GUILLAUME
With half-pay of 6 livres per month, according to a decision of September 8, 1770.
DU BEAU, CLAUDE AUGUSTIN
With half-pay of 6 livres per month according to a decision of April 4, 1764, sent to the Bureau des Invalides April 5, 1764.
DUBOIS, HENRY
Discharged November 30, 1769, roll of January 1, 1763, folio 46
DUBOIS, JACQUES JOSEPH
Discharged February 6, 1770, company of Duplessis.
DUBOIS, JEAN
Ruturned from prison in England. Debarked at Boulogne. His passport was visaed at the Bureau June 9, 1763, to go to Rochefort where he will embark to return to Louisiana to rejoin his wife and children.
DUBOIS, JEAN
Discharged. See the roll of the Same day, May 2, 1763.
DUBOIS, JEAN BAPTISTE
Discharged May 1, 1751.
DUBOIS, JACQUES JOSEPH
DUBOIS, PIERRE
DU BOIS, RENÉ DE LA CHAMBRE
Died March 6, 1750.
DUBRAS, PIERRE
Discharged September 15, 1763, roll of January 1, 1763, folio 13.

LOUISIANA TROOPS —:— 1720-1770

DU BREUIL, JEAN
Deserted August 20, 1751.

DUBUISSON, DOMINIQUE
Killed himself by a gun blast at La Balize February 11, 1759. See the roll of June 1, 1760, folio 4.

DUBUISSON, FRANCOIS

DU BUISSON, JOSEPH
Died August 5, 1751.

DUBUT, JACQUES
With half-pay of 9 livres per month, according to a decision of June 11, 1764, sent to the Bureau des Invalides the same day.

DUC, JOSEPH
Discharged February 1, 1751.

DUCHEF, JEAN BAPTISTE
Discharged March 11, 1757.

DUCHEMIN, SEBASTIEN
Died at Natchez, March 29, 1759, company of Dorgon.

DU CHESNE, ANTOINE FRANCOIS
Discharged May 16, 1754.

DUCOUSSEAU, JOSEPH
Died at Akancas December 21, 1754, company of Hazeur.

DUCRÉ, ARMAND LOUIS
Discharged October 30, 1756.

DUCROS, JEAN
Discharged June 26, 1751.

DUCROZ, JOSEPH
Discharged March 1, 1751.

DUCUIR, LAURENT

DUCUIRE, LAURENT
Discharged September 15, 1763, roll of January 1, 1763, folio 24.

DUDOIGT, PIERRE FRANCOIS
Deserted November 15, 1761. See the roll of the same year, folio 16.

DUFFAUD, PIERRE
Discharged September 15, 1763, roll of January 1, 1763, folio 25.

DUFAYE, ETIENNE
Drowned February 7, 1766, roll of January 1, 1763, folio 33.

DUFORT JEAN

DUFORT, JEAN
Discharged in Louisiana November 20, 1769, with half-pay of 9 livres per month, according to a decision of April 28, 1770.

DUFOSSAT, GUY
Cadet Soldat. Died August 24, 1756, company of Aubry.

DUFOUR, JACQUES AUGUSTIN
Discharged and went to France on the Messager.

DUFOUR, NICOLAS
Died at the hospital at New Orleans, September 26, 1769, roll of January 1, 1763, folio 44.

DUFRESNE, JEAN OLLIVIER
Discharged October 1, 1764, roll of January 1, 1763, folio 29.

DUHARD, MARTIN
Died December 7, 1751.

DUMAIN, FRANCOIS
Sergeant. With half-pay of 9 livres per month according to a decision of November 30, 1764, sent to the Bureau des Invalides December 1, 1764. Discharged July 1, 1764.

DUMANCHE, PIERRE

DU MECHE, ETIENNE
Died January 9, 1750.

DUMESNIL, FRANCOIS
Died September 12, 1757, company of D'Hauterive.

DUMENSIL, LOUIS

DUMOUTIER, ISAIE
Discharged August 20, 1770, requested half-pay. See the decision of September 8, 1776, in the carton of half-pay (papers). June 9, 1777, he was given half-pay of 6 livres per month. See the decision of the same day.

DUNANT, JEAN BAPTISTE

DUNANT, PIERRE

DUNOT, JOSEPH

DUPART, CLAUDE
Died at Mobile November 30, 1775, company of Marentin.

LOUISIANA TROOPS —:— 1720-1770

DUPAS, JEAN
　Died at Natchez September 1, 1758. See the roll of June 1, 1760, folio 8.
DUPASQUIER, HENRY
　Went to France on the Samson, October 1, 1769, roll of January 1, 1763, folio 45.
DUPERET, CLAUDE LOUIS
　Discharged September 15, 1763, roll of January 1, 1763, folio 12.
DUPLANUE, JEAN PIERRE
　Died February 25, 1756, company of Marentin.
DUPRÉ, FRANCOIS
　Deserted July 19, 1755.
DUPRÉ, JEAN
　Deserted June 8, 1755.
DUPRÉ, JEAN BAPTISTE
　Engaged in 1762. Discharged October 8, 1769, roll of January 1, 1763, folio 55.
DUPUY, BERNARD
　Deserted the latter part of June, 1751.
DUPUY, FRANCOIS
DURAND, ANTOINE
　Drowned in the sinking of the Pere de Famille February 17, 1770, returning to France.
DURAND, FRANCOIS
　Engaged in 1762. Discharged October 8, 1769, roll of January 1, 1763, folio 55.

DURAND, JACQUES
　Discharged February 6, 1770, with half-pay of 4 livres 10 sols per month, according to a decision of April 28, 1770.
DURAND, JACQUES
　Discharged permanently and went to France on the royal vessel Fortune January 1, 1759. See the roll of June 1, 1760, folio 8.
DURAND, JEAN
DURAND, JOSEPH
DURAND, LOUIS ANTOINE
　Discharged September 15, 1763, roll of January 1 1763, folio 6.
DURIE, FRANCOIS DOMINIQUE
　Discharged June 15, 1756.
DU SOULIER, ANTOINE
　Discharged June 1, 1751.
DU TILLET, Lè Sieur
DUTISNEE, PIERRE
　Cadet. Died October 8, 1750.
DUVARDET, CLAUDE
　Deserted August 1, 1758. See the roll of June 1, 1760, folio 8.
DUVARDET, CLAUDE
　Deserted August 1, 1758. See the roll of June 1, 1760, folio 8.
DUVERT, JEAN
DUVILLARD, JACQUES
　Discharged October 8, 1769, roll of January 1, 1763, folio 43.

EDELING, JEAN
EDLÉ, FRANCOIS
    Went to France on the Samson, October 1, 1769, roll of January 11, 1763, folio 52.
EDMÉ, MATHIEU
    Discharged September 15, 1763, roll of January 1, 1763, folio 12.
EDOUIN ANTOINE
    Discharged September 15, 1763, roll of January 1, 1763, folio 8.
EGAND, JEAN BAPTISTE
    Dischaged September 30, remained at Natchitoches, roll of January 1, 1763, folio 48.

ELIBON, PIERRE
    Discharged September 15, 1763, roll of January 1, 1763, folio 7.
EMERY, JACQUES FRANCOIS
ERAME, LOUIS
ESCOUDER, JACQUES
ESPINET, JEAN BAPTISTE
    Discharged November 30, 1769, roll of January 1, 1763, folio 44.
EXCROUSAILLES, ANTOINE
    Discharged April 18, 1756. Went to France on the vessel La Messager.

LOUISIANA TROOPS —:— 1720-1770

FABRE, PIERRE
Died at the hospital July 26, 1763, roll of January 1, 1763, folio 19.

FABRY, LOUIS ALEXANDRE
Discharged May 1, 1754, company of Derneville.

FAIFFRE, JEAN

FAILHET, JACQUES
Major drummer. Discharged August 18, 1751.

FAILLARD, JEAN

FALCON, GERMAIN
Discharged November 30, 1769 roll of January 1, 1763, folio 53.

FALCONNET, CLAUDE
Discharged June 25, 1751.

FANTON, LOUIS
Discharged November 30, 1769, roll of January 1, 1763, folio 49.

FARINEAU, MARTIN

FARON, PIERRE
Discharged September 15, 1763, roll of January 1, 1763, folio 8.

FARQUET, AIMEE
Deserted at the Balize August 30, 1761. See the roll of the same year, folio 43.

FAUCHÉ, ANTOINE
Corporal. With half-pay of 8 livres per month, according to a decision of April 4, 1764, sent to the Bureau des Invalides, April 5, 1764.

FAUCHÉ, CLAUDE
He was drowned and was found by the Indians, June 5, 1751.

FAUPIED, JEAN
Deserted June 19, 1758. See the roll of June 1, 1760, folio 6.

FAUSS, FREDERIC
Discharged February 6, 1770, company of Duplessis.

FAUVIN, FRANCOIS
Died at the hospital September 16, 1755, company of Montberault.

FAVELIER, ANTOINE

FAVET, LOUIS

FAVET, LOUIS
with his wife and two children, drowned in the sinking of the Pere de Famille February 17, 1770, returning to France.

FAVIER, GUILLEAUME
Discharged April 18, 1756. He went to France.

FAVRE, JEAN

FAVRE, PIERRE
Corporal. With half-pay of 12 livres per month according to a decision of April 26, 1766, sent to the Bureau des Invalides April 27, 1766.

FAVRE, PIERRE
Discharged September 15, 1763, roll of January 1, 1763, folio 5.

FTYE ETIENNE FRANCOIS
Discharged August 18, 1751.

FELKER, JACQUES
Drowned descending from Natchez October 28, 1754, company of Grandpre.

FELMAN, LAURENT
Discharged September 30, 1769, roll of January 1, 1763, folio 45.

FENARD, JEAN PIERRE
Discharged July 31, 1764, roll of January 1, 1763, folio 27. Discharged July 26, 1756.

FENOUILLOT, CLAUDE

FENOUILLOT, JEAN CLAUDE

FERAND, FRANCOIS
Discharged February 6, 1770, with half-pay of 4 livres 10 sols according to a decision of April 28, 1770.

FERRAND, FRANCOIS

FERRANT, JEAN

FERRARE or FERRARIE, PROSPER
Sergeant. With half-pay of 12 livres per month according to a decision of April 4, 1764, sent to the Bureau des Invalides April 5, 1764. Discharged September 15, 1763.

FERRARY, PROSPER

FERRAUD, FIACRE

FERRÉ, FRANCOIS
Deserted April 28, 1750.

LOUISIANA TROOPS —:— 1720-1770

FERRÉ, JEAN FIRMIN
Discharged March 1, 1764, roll of January 1, 1763, folio 30.

FERRET, FRANCOIS
Died May 27, 1734, death certificate in proper form at the Bureau des Invalides.

FERRET, PIERRE
FERRETTE, HYACINTHE FERRET
Discharged June 30, 1768, roll of January 1, 1763 folio 36.

FERRETTE, MARC

FERRIN, MICHEL JOSEPH
Drowned in the sinking of the Pere de Famille February 17, 1770, returning to France.

FESTE, JOSEPH
Deserted August 30, 1761. See the roll of the same year, folio 46.

FEUGET, PIERRE
Discharged September 15, 1763, roll of January 1, 1763, folio 13.

FICHÉ, JOSEPH
Died September 15, 1750.

FICHER, PIERRE

FIGUERRE, JEAN BAPTISTE
Deserted September 25, 1755.

FIGUERRE, JEAN BAPTISTE
Extended leave issued. He went to France on the royal vessel Fortune January 1, 1759. See the roll of June 1, 1760, folio 5.

FILON, MATHIEU
With half-pay of 6 livres per month according to a decision of April 4, 1764, sent to the Bureau des Invalides April 5, 1764, discharged September 15, 1763, roll of January 1, 1763, folio 4.

FILOSA, SYLVAIN

FINET, JOSEPH HUBERT
Discharged September 15, 1763, roll of January 1, 1763, folio 4 (?).

FITON, MATHIEU

FITTE, JEAN
Discharged September 30, 1769, roll of January 1, 1763, folio 54.

FIZELLE, REYNARD
Died at the hospital June 26, 1765, roll of January 1, 1763, folio 32.

FLAMAND, JEAN
Died October 31, 1735, death certificate in proper form at the Bureau des Invalides.

FLAMANT, PIERRE
Sergeant. Hanged September 10, 1753. See the criminal proceedings in the Louisiana file.

FLAMBARD, PIERRE

FLAMIEN, FRANCOIS
Discharged September 15, 1763, roll of January 1, 1763, folio 20.

FLAMIER, JOSEPH
Died September 1, 1738, death certificate in proper form at the Bureau des Invalides.

FLAURE, JOSEPH LAURENT
Deserted July 17, 1751.

FLECHY, PIERRE
Died January 8, 1746, Company of Gaumet.

FLEURY, CLAUDE

FLEURY, CLAUDE
Discharged February 6, 1770, with half-pay of 4 livres 10 sols per month according to a decision of April 28, 1770.

FLORÉS, NICOLAS

FLOUARD, PIERRE
Discharged September 15, 1763, roll of January 1, 1763, folio 23.

FOIRÉ, PIERRE
Corporal. Discharged February 6, 1770, with half-pay of 15 livres per month according to a decision of April 28, 1770.

FOL, JULIEN DENIS
With half-pay of 6 livres per month according to a decision of April 4, 1764, sent to the Bureau des Invalides Auril 5, 1764.

FOLTRAY, ANTOINE

FONDEUR, JEAN PIERRE
Discharged November 1, 1764, roll of January 1, 1763, folio 28.

LOUISIANA TROOPS —:— 1720-1770

FONDEUR or FONDAIR or FONDEUX, JEAN PIERRE
With half-pay of 6 lires per month, according to a decision of March 22, 1765, sent to the Bureau des Invalides.

FONTAINE, ANTOINE

FONTAINE, GERMAIN
Drowned in the sinking of the Pere de Famille February 17, 1770, returning to France.

FONTAINE, HENRY
Discharged March 1, 1764, roll of January 1, 1763, folio 28.

FONTENAY, ABRAHAM
Died at Natchez July 29, 1754, company of La Gautraye.

FONTENEAU, FRANCOIS
Died at Mobile, January 16, 1759, see the roll of June 1, 1760, folio 12.

FONTENEAU, HENRY
Discharged September 15, 1763, roll of January 1, 1763, folio 26.

FONTENEAU, JEAN

FONTENEAU, JEAN LOUIS
Died at Alibamons October 29, 1755, company of Grandchamp.

FONTENEAU, JEAN LOUIS
Engaged January 1, 1743. Discharged September 15, 1763, roll of January 1, 1763, folio 11.

FONTENEAU, JOSEPH
With half-pay of 4 livres 10 sols, according to a decision of Jue 11, 1764, sent to the Bureau des Invalides June 12, 1764. Discharged September 15, 1763.

FONTENEAU, LOUIS

FONTENEAU, PHILIPPES
With half-pay of 6 livres per month, according to a decision of June 11, 1764, sent to the Bureau des Invalides June 12, 1764. Discharged September 15, 1763.

FONTENEAU, PIERRE

FONTENEAU, PIERRE
Discharged September 15, 1763, roll of January 1, 1763, folio 5.

FONTINELLE, JEAN BAPTISTE
Died October 10, 1751.

FORESTIER, LOUIS NICOLAS
Discharged at Rochefort, June 6, 1761, and presented his permanent discharge at the Bureau September 11, 1761, with half-pay of 6 livres per month, sent to the Bureau des Invalides December 12, 1761.

FORGEUR, JOSEPH

FORNERET, LOUIS
Discharged September 15, 1763, roll of January 1, 1763, folio 10.

FORT, JEAN PIERRE
Discharged July 16, 1756, went to France.

FOSSE, ROBERT
Deserted at Illinois in 1755

FOUBERT, FRANCOIS
Discharged September 15, 1763, roll of January 1, 1763, folio 22.

FOUCAULT, JACQUES
With half-pay of 9 livres per month according to a decision of May 25, 1764, sent to the Bureau des Invalides. Discharged September 15, 1763, roll of January 1, 1763, folio 2.

FOUCAULT, PIERRE
With half-pay of 6 livres per month, according to a decision of January 28, 1766, sent to the Bureau des Invalides January 29, 1766. Discharged July 1, 1765.

FOUDOIX, JACQUES

FOUILLOT, PIERRE
Went to the Cap on the vessel La Concorde, December 15, 1754.

FOUQUET, ANTOINE
Died at the hospital, October 13, 1756, company of Derneville.

FOURCADE, BERNARD

LOUISIANA TROOPS —:— 1720-1770

FOURCHAUD, FRANCOIS
Discharged December 31, 1764, roll of January 1, 1763, folio 28. He was re-engaged April 16, 1769, discharged October 8, 1769; see the same roll, folio 55.

FOURCHET, JEAN
Killed by the Indians, August 1, 1754, company of Orgon.

FOURÉ, LOUIS
Discharged September 15, 1763, roll of January 1, 1763 folio 9.

FOURÉ, PIERRE

FOURNIER, ANTOINE
Extended leave. He went to France on the royal vessel La Fortune, January 1, 1759. See the roll of June 1, 1760, folio 10.

FOURNIER, JEAN
Died March 10, 1751.

FOURNIER, JEAN
Died December 23, 1736, death certificate in proper form at the Bureau des Invalides.

FOURNIER, JEAN FRANCOIS
Died at Arkancas May 20, 1759. See the roll of June 1, 1760, folio 5.

FOURQUEUX, JEAN BAPTISTE
Discharged March 1, 1751, to become a habitant.

FOYER, JEAN

FOYER, JEAN
Discharged February 6, 1770, with half-pay of 4 livres 10 sols per month according to a decision of April 28, 1770.

FRANC, JEAN

FRANC, JEAN

FRANCOIS, DOMINIQUE
Died at New Orleans January 19, 1768, roll of January 1, 1763, folio 35.

FRANCOIS, LOUIS
Condemned to the gallies for life, February 9, 1756.

FRANCOIS, PIERRE
Invalid. Discharged, company of Organ.

FRANCURE, VILLERS
Discharged the latter part of April, 1751.

FRAUDON, DENIS
Discharged August 18, 1751.

FREAN, JEAN BAPTISTE
Deserted in May, 1756.

FRECHENE, VICTOR
Died, company of Marest. The date of his death is not on the roll.

FREDERIC, JEAN
Drummer.

FREDERIK, JEAN
With half-pay of 6 livres per month from April 4, 1764, sent to the Bureau des Invalides April 5, 1764. Discharged September 15, 1768.

FREINT, JEAN
Deserted July 17, 1755, and condemned by contumacy to be hung July 19, 1755.

FRESNEAU, JEAN FRANCOIS
Discharged April 1, 1767, roll of January 1, 1763, folio 24.

FRICHARD, JEAN
Discharged September 15, 1763, roll of January 1, 1763, folio 22.

FRITOT, MICHEL

FROMENTIN, NICOLAS PIERRE
Discharged July 1, 1764, roll of January 1, 1763, folio 29.

GABARIAU, MATHURIN
Died November 9, 1754, company of Mazan.

GABET, CLAUDE FRANCOIS
Discharged May 1, 1767, roll of January 1, 1763, folio 35

GABORY, SIGIBERT LEOPOL

GABORY, SIGISBERT LEOPOL
Discharged at Isle of Re August 20, 1770, with half-pay of 9 livres per month according to a decision of October 17, 1770.

GABRIEL, CHARLES

GAGNON, PHILIBERT

GAILLARD, JEAN
Drummer. Died at the hospital February 23, 1763, roll of January 1, 1763, folio 16.

GALANNE, PIERRE
Deserted March 30, 1755.

GALLARD, ETIENNE

GALLART, ETIENNE
Discharged February 6, 1770, company of Villiers.

GALLET, ROBERT

GALLOIS, MICHEL
Discharged April 18, 1756, went to France.

GALOPEINS, ANTOINE

GAMIN, PIERRE
Died October 11, 1751.

GANDOIT, PIERRE
Died at the hospital May 31, 1766, roll of January 1, 1763, folio 33.

GANGAN, LOUIS
Died October 13, 1751.

GANIER, LOUIS
Discharged September 15, 1763, roll of January 1, 1763, folio 21.

GARAY, BARTHELEMY
Discharged July 26, 1756.

GARCIN, FRANCOIS
With half-pay of 4 livres 10 sols per month according to a decision of April 4, 1764, sent to the Bureau des Invalides April 5, 1764. Discharged September 15, 1763.

GAREL, CHARLES
Died. Company of Grandpre. The date of his death is not on the roll sent in 1746.

GARILLON, BLAIZE

GARILLON, BLAIZE
Drowned in the sinking of the Pere de Famille February 17, 1770, returning to France.

GARNIER, LAURENT

GARY, BARTHELEMY
Died at the hospital December 13, 1756, company of Grandpre.

GASQUIN, ETIENNE DENIS

GAUDET, JEAN
Corporal. Discharged September 15, 1763. With half-pay of 9 livres per month since April 4, 1764, sent to the Bureau des Invalides April 5, 1764, payable to Autun in Bourgogne.

GAUDET, JEAN
Corporal. With half-pay of 9 livres per month according to a decision of September 8, 1770.

GAUDOT, AGNAN
Died December 29, 1751.

GAUDIER, FRANCOIS
Discharged October 18, 1764, roll of January 1, 1763, folio 27.

GAUDIN, SIMON
Drowned at Ouabache November 19, 1756, company of Macarty.

GAULARD, FRANCOIS LOUIS
Died September 14, 1751.

GAUTHIER, FRANCOIS

GAUTIER, ANTOINE
Dismissed (chassé) June 24 1769, roll of January 1, 1763, folio 51.

GAUTIER, FRANCOIS
Discharged February 6, 1770, with half-pay of 6 livres per month according to a decision of April 28, 1770. Corporal.

GAUTIER, NICOLAS
With half-pay of 6 livres per month according to a decision of April 4, 1764, sent to the Bureau des Invalides April 5, 1764. Discharged September 15, 1763. Corporal.

LOUISIANA TROOPS —:— 1720-1770

GAUTIER, RENÉ
Died April 25, 1758. See the roll of June 1, 1760, folio 3.

GELOIX, CAESAR
Died at the hospital July 16, 1756, company of Grandchamp.

GENAY or GENET, JOSEPH
Died at the hospital October 12, 1766, roll of January 1, 1763, folio 33.

GENNEVOIS, JEAN
Deserted July 29, 1751.

GENTY, CLAUDE
Discharged September 15, 1763, roll of January 1, 1763, folio 16 (or 96).

GENTY, EDME ROMAIN
Drowned descending from Natchez October 2, 1754, company of Artuad.

GENTY, JEAN

GEORGES, DOMINIQUE
Lost June 27, 1765, roll of January 1, 1763 folio 31.

GEORGES, FRANCOIS
Deserted July 4, 1755.

GEORGES, JEAN
Discharged September 30, 1769, roll of January 1763 folio 48.

GEORGES, JEAN BAPTISTE
Died July 30, 1755, company of Orgon.

GERARD, ANTOINE

GERARD, EDMÉ
With half-pay of 6 livres per month according to a decision of April 4, 1764, sent to the Bureau des Invalides April 5, 1764. Discharged September 15, 1743.

GERARD, JOSEPH
Killed at Mobile July 11, 1757, company of Bellenos.

GERARD, LOUIS
Died November 7, 1751.

GERARD, MICHEL
Discharged May 1, 1751.

GERARD, PHILIPPES
With half-pay of 6 livres per month according to a decision of April 4, 1764, sent to the Bureau des Invalides April 5, 1764. Discharged September 15, 1763.

GERARD, SIMON
Discharged September 1, 1756.

GERARDIN, JEAN
Discharged September 15, 1763, roll of January 1, 1763, folio 22.

GERBEAU, JACQUES
Discharged July 22, 1751.

GERBIER, ETIENNE
Died May 15, 1755, company of Marentin.

GERMAIN, ETIENNE
Died April 17, 1751.

GERMAIN, JEAN

GERMAIN, JEAN
Fusileer. Discharged August 20, 1770, with half-pay of 6 livres per month.

GESCOTE, FRANCOIS
Died at the hospital September 23, 1754 company of Trant.

GESNE, TOUSSAINT
Discharged August 19, 1756, company of La Tour.

GIBAUT, JOSEPH
Died in Illinois December 1, 1755,, company of Marentin.

GILBERT, ANTOINE
Died August 7, 1744, company of Membrede.

GILBERT, FRANCOIS
Died April 29, 1750.

GILBERT, JEAN

GILBERT, JEAN
Drowned in the sinking of the Pere de Famille, February 17, 1770, returning to France.

GILBERT, JEAN
Discharged September 15, 1763, roll of January 1, 1763, folio 11.

GILBERT, JEROSME
Died at the hospital November 27, 1758. See the roll of June 1, 1760, folio 10.

GILLART, SEBASTIAN
Deserted June 8, 1755.

GILLET, FRANCOIS
Died September 14, 1751.

GIMMEVAL, JEAN

GIRARD, ANDRÉ
Discharged July 1, 1767, roll of January 1, 1763, folio 34.

GIRARD, JOSEPH
Deserted September 27, 1754.

GIRAUD, JEAN FRANCOIS
Drowned at Ouabache November 10, 1756, company of Desmazellieres.

GIRAUD, SIMON

GIRAULT, RENE

GIRAY, JACQUES
Died at Mobile November 4, 1758. See the roll of June 1, 1760, folio 3.

GIROND, NICOLAS
Discharged September 15, 1763, roll of January 1, 1763, folio 1.

GIROND, PIERRE
Deserted August 29, 1757. Condemned by contumacy to be shot, according to a judgement of April 24, 1758. See the roll of June 1, 1761, folio 10.

GISCLAIRE, JEAN
Discharged September 15, 1763, roll of January 1, 1763, folio 18.

GIVOTEAU, GUILLAUME
See Pivoteau in the "P" section. Discharged September 15, 1763, roll of January 1, 1763, folio 5.

GIVRY, DENIS
Drowned in the river. The roll sent December 24, 1758, makes no mention of the year in which he drowned. He was of the company of Arazola.

GLACHAUD or GLANCHAUD, LOUIS

GLAINET (GLAMET?), FRANCOIS

GLAIRE, ABRAHAM
Deserted August 30, 1761. See the roll of the same year, folio 43.

GODART, LAURENT
Discharged September 15, 1763, roll of January 1, 1763, folio 9.

GODART, LOUIS
See the list of Monsieur de Repentigny for February 6, 1770.

GODEAUX, DESIRÉ
Discharged. See the roll dated at Calais May 2, 1763.

GODIN, ANDRÉ
Died December 25, 1750.

GOGUÉ, JOSEPH
With half-pay of 6 livres per month according to a decision of April 4, 1764, sent to the Bureau des Invalides April 5, 1764. Discharged September 15, 1763.

GOIFEARD, BENOIST
Discharged September 15, 1763, roll of January 1, 1763, folio 15.

GOLESSEAU, MATHIEU
Drowned at Tombekbe April 27, 1755, company of La Tour.

GOLLEMART, JEAN

GONARD, ETIENNE
Taken (prisoner) by the English in 1754, returning to Louisiana, and was not returned to France until April 26, 1762. Discharged at Rochefort May 16, 1762. He was a sergeant. Thirty livres of travel money, which he did not receive, to go to Tonnere (?).

GONIN, ABRAHAM

GONIN, JEAN
Died at New Orleans March 22, 1768, roll of January 1, 1763, folio 35.

GONISCH, CLAUDE
Died December 20, 1735. Death certificate in porper order at the Bureau des Invalides.

GONOT, JEAN
Deserted February 5, 1739.

GONS, JOSEPH
Discharged February 6, 1770, company of Duplessis

LOUISIANA TROOPS —:— 1720-1770

GONZALLES, ANTOINE
Discharged September 15, 1763, roll of January 1, 1763, folio 10.

GORNOVILLE, FRANCOIS
Entered service June 1, 1769. Discharged November 30, 1769.

GOSSELIN, JACQUES

GOSSELIN, JEAN

GOSSON, ANTOINE

GOTIFFIER, CLAUDE

GOUFFIER, JEAN FRANCOIS

GOUJARD, FRANCOIS
Sergeant. With half-pay of 12 livres per month according to a decision of April 5, 1764. Discharged September 15, 1763.

GOULIAT, BENOIST
Deserted February 15, 1750.

GOUPY, DENIS
Licensed at Havre in February of 1761. See the general roll of that port for February 22, 1761, folio 5.

GOUPY, GEORGES

GOURLIER, ANTOINE
Discharged September 15, 1763. Roll of January 1, 1763, folio 19.

GOUTTE, PIERRE
Died August 27, 1751.

GOVARE, PHILIPPES MARIE

GOYAUX, NICOLAS
Drowned at the Balize January 10, 1754, company of Macarty.

GOYEUX, JEAN
Deserted February 5, 1739.

GRANDCHAMP, LOUIS

GRANDPRES, ADRIEN
Discharged Septmeber 15, 1763, roll of January 1, 1763, folio 18.

GRAFINEAU, PAUL
Drowned November 1, 1738. Death certificate in proper order at the Bureau des Invalide.

GRAILLOT, CHARLES
Discharged April 18, 1756, went to France.

GRAPPE, ALEXIS
Discharged September 15, 1763, roll of January 1, 1763, folio 25.

GRASSIN FRANCOIS
Drowned descending from Akancas February 14, 1755, company of Reggio.

GREVETAUT, NICOLAS FRANCOIS
With half-pay of 6 livres per month according to a decision of April 4, 1764, sent to the Bureau des Invalides April 5, 1764.

GREMINGUE, JEROSME
Deserted April 29, 1751.

GREMOT, SIMON

GREMPEL, SIMON
Died October 21, 1751.

GRENADE, NICOLAS
Drummer. With half-pay of 6 livres per month according to a decision of April 4, 1764, sent o the Bureau des Invalides April 5, 1764. Discharged September 15, 1763.

GRENET, ANTOINE
Discharged September 30, 1769, roll of January 1, 1763, folio 50.

GRENIER, JEAN BAPTISTE
Discharged September 15, 1763, roll of January 1, 1763, folio 26.

GRENIER LOUIS
With half-play of 6 livres per month according to a decision of April 4 1764, sent to the Bureau des Invalides April 5, 1764. Discharged September 15, 1763.

GRENIER, PIERRE
Died October 17, 1750.

GRENOUVILLE, FRANCOIS
Habitant since February 22, 1753.

GREVÉ or GRENÉ, VINCENT
Died July 26, 1734. Death certificate in proper form at the Buerau des Invalides.

GRIEL, PAUL

GRIEN, FRANTZ (?) THIBAULT
Discharged September 30, 1769, roll of January 1, 1763, folio 54

GRILLET, MARIN

GRILLOT (or) GRILLAUD, LAZARRE
Discharged August 10, 1751.

GRIMPEL, SIMON

GRINON, MICHEL ANTOINE
Discharged June 20, 1756.

GRISON, FRANCOIS
Died November 6, 1750.

GRISSON, JOSEPH
Discharged July 17, 1756.

GROGNET, ANTOINE

GROMMÉ, JEAN
Died October 2, 1735. Death certificate in proper order at the Bureau des Invalides.

GRONIETE, ANTOINE
Discharged September 15, 1763, roll of January 1 1763, folio 5.

GROS, BARTHELEMY
Drowned August 1, 1751

GROS-JACQUES, JEAN PIERRE
Killed by the Indians at Riviere Cherakis July 4, 1757, company of Desvarennes.

GROSSON or GOSSON, ANTOINE
Discharged September 15, 1763, roll of January 1, 1763, folio 14.

GRUEL, PIERRE
Died December 2, 1736. Death certificate in proper order at the Bureau des Invalides.

GRUISSES, CHARLES
Died September 28, 1769, roll of January 1, 1763, folio 54.

GUARBE, JOSEPH
Died at the hospital July 19, 1767, roll of January 1, 1763, folio 34.

GUAY, JEAN BAPTISTE
Died April 22 1751.

GUÉ, JOSEPH
Deserted July 13, 1750

GUENAUT, JACQUES LAURENT
Discharged September 15, 1763, roll of January 1, 1763, folio 12.

GUENON, JEAN BAPTISTE
Died July 13, 1758. See the roll of June 1, 1760, folio 10.

GUENON, JOSEPH
With half-pay of 6 livres per month according to a decision of April 4, 1764, sent to the Bureau des Invalides April 5, 1764.

GUERAULT, BERNARD
Deserted September 17, 1756.

GUERIN, GUILLAUME

GUERIN, GUILLAUME
Re-engaged.

GUERIN, JEAN
Discharged May 1, 1751.

GUERIN, JEAN
Discharged October 31, 1769, roll of January 1, 1763, folio 46.

GUERIN, JEAN LOUIS
Drowned ascending to Natchez December 19, 1754, company of Sommes.

GUERIN, MARTIN

GUERLOT, REMY

GUERPIN, JEAN BAPTISTE

GUERPIN, JEAN BAPTISTE
Discharged August 20, 1770, with half-pay of 6 livres per month according to a decision of October 17, 1770.

GUERRAULT, BERNARD
Deserted September 17, 1756.

GUERRE, JOSEPH

GUERRY, PIERRE
Died at Akancas, December 22, 1754, company of Mazan.

GUESDON, JEAN
Discharged July 25, 1768, roll of Jan. 1, 1763, folio 36.

GUESNIER, GILLES
Died in August, 1754, company of Mazan.

GUESNON, PIERRE

GUIBILLON, PIERRE
Deserted September 17, 1754.

GUICHARD, JACQUES

GUIDON, JOSEPH
Died September 10, 1734. Death certificate in proper form at the Bureau des Invalides.

GUIGNE, PIERRE
Discharged February 6, 1770, company of Villiers.

GUIGNON, JACQUES
Died suddenly April 11, 1756. Discharged invalide, company of Murat.

GUILGAU, JEAN
Discharged August 1, 1750.

GUILLARD, LOUIS
Died December 17, 1750.

GUILLARD, LOUIS
Dismissed (Chassé) September 30, 1769, roll of January 1, 1763, folio 53.

GUILLEAUME, DENIS
Drowned in the river July 22, 1769, roll of January 1, 1763, folio 50.

GUILLEMARIE, FRANCOIS
Died October 16, 1751.

GUILLET, PIERRE
Discharged October 16, 1764, roll of January 1, 1763, folio 27.

GUILLOCHEAUD, PIERRE
Discharged September 1, 1758, and went to France on the royal vessel La Fortune January 1, 1759. See the roll of June 1, 1760, folio 10.

GUILLOT, ENNEMOND
Discharged February 1, 1766, roll of January 1, 1763, folio 33.

GUILLOT, PIERRE
Died October 18, 1751

GUILLOTEAU, JACQUES
Sergeant. Discharged March 31, 1761. See the roll of the same year, folio 12. With half-pay of 10 livres per month according to a decision of April 4, 1764, sent to the Bureau des Invalides April 5, 1764

GUILLOTEAU, JACQUES PHILIPE

GUILLOTON, FRANCOIS
Died April 17, 1763, roll of January 1, 1763, folio 9.

GUILMER, JEAN BAPTISTE
Died at the hospital November 7, 1757, company of Orgon.

GUIMAUD, HENRY
Discharged September 15, 1763, roll of January 1, 1763, folio 12.

GUIMEAU or GUIMAUD, CLAUDE
Discharged September 15, 1763, roll of January 1, 1763, folio 11.

GUINARD, HENRY
With half-pay of 6 livres per month according to a decision of April 4, 1764, sent to the Bureau des Invalides April 5, 1764.

GUINAUD, F. VICTOR
GUINAULT, VICTOR
Discharged July 16, 1754, went to France.

GUINCHARD, ETIENNE
Discharged October 31, 1769, roll of January 1, 1763, folio 38.

GUINET, CLAUDE AUGUSTIN
Died November 5, 1734. Death certificate in proper form at the Bureau des Invalides.

GUINET, LAURENT
Deserted April 30, 1756.

GUINET, PIERRE

GUINOT, JOSEPH
Discharged September 15, 1763, roll of January 1, 1763, folio 10.

GUIOT, FRANCOIS
Died at the hospital September 25, 1756, company of Desmazellieres.

GUYOT, CHARLES
Deserted February 28, 1750.

GUYOT, RENÉ JACQUES
Died July 8, 1745, company of Gauvry.

LOUISIANA TROOPS —:— 1720-1770

HAIDILAI, FRANCOIS
Company of Villiers. Discharged February 6, 1770.

HANN, FRANCOIS
Engaged July 1, 1768. Discharged October 8, 1769, roll of January 1, 1763, folio 55.

HAQUET, EDME
Died at the hospital January 13, 1759. See the roll of June 1, 1760, folio 10.

HAQUIN, JACQUES

HARAULT, PIERRE

HARDY, NOEL JOSEPH

HARDY, PIERRE
Discharged September 15, 1763, roll of January 1, 1763, folio 12.

HARLAY, JEAN BAPTISTE
With half-pay of 6 livres per month according to a decision of April 4, 1764, sent to the Bureau des Invalides April 5, 1764. Discharged September 15, 1763.

HARMENSTRAND, Mr.
From London, lieutenant-colonel in the service of England. Drowned in the sinking of the Pere de Famille February 17, 1770, returning to France

HARQUET, JEAN
Died October 11, 1751.

HAVARD, LOUIS
Died October 25, 1751.

HEBERT, ADRIEN
Discharged March 1, 1766, roll of January 1, 1763, folio 33

HEBREMAN, GEORGES

HELK, MICHEL
Company of Vaugine. Discharged February 6, 1770.

HELOT, LOUIS

HENNEQUIN, NICOLAS
Discharged September 15, 1763, roll of January 1, 1763, folio 1.

HENRY, ANTOINE
Died at Mobile December 4, 1756, company of Montberault. August 22, 1762, dispatched his death certificate and delivered it the same day to Monsieur Charpentier of the Bureau fonds de la marine.

HENRY, JACQUES

HENRY, JEAN
Died at the hospital January 5, 1755, company of Artuad.

HENRY, JEAN BAPTISTE
Sergeant of the detachment of artillery serving in Louisiana. Discharged March 10, 1769. He presented his discharge to the Bureau with half-pay of 15 livres per month according to a decision of June 18, 1769, sent to the Bureau des Invalides.

HENRY, PASCAL
Executed by the firing squad July 30, 1751.

HERBELAY, HUBERT
Died at the hospital September 10, 1755, company of Grandpre.

HERBERT, JEAN
Killed or taken prisoner at Fort Ouabache by the Cherakis or Chicachas November 9, 1757, company of Chabert.

HERIER, CLAUDE

HERMANE, (?) JOSEPH

HERSAN, JEAN FRANCOIS
Deserted October 17, 1765. Condemned to be shot following a judgement by contumacy dated Louisiana, October 17, 1765.

HERVE, FRANCOIS

HERVIEUX, CLAUDE

HERVY, CHARLES

HERVY, JACQUES
Died December 22, 1750.

HIBOU, DONAT
Discharged August 10, 1756

HIBY, THIBAULT
Deserted February 5, 1739.

HIERLE, FRANCOIS
Discharged July 1, 1750.

HIPPOL, JEAN

HIRTZ, JEAN PIERRE
Drummer, company of Mazilliere. Discharged February 6, 1770.

HIRAULT, JACQUES
Discharged September 15, 1763, roll of January 1, 1763, folio 6.

HODABLE, ALEXANDRE
See the "O" section.

HODIER ANDRÉ
Invalide. Discharged.

HOMFROY, CHARLES GUILLAUME

HORÉ, JEAN
Died at Natchitoches March 3, 1755, company of Chabert.

HOTZ, MENARD
Discharged July 16, 1754.

HOUCK, ANDRÉ
Deserted July 19, 1755, and condemned by contumacy to be hanged.

HOUSSET, PIERRE
Discharged September 15, 1763, roll of January 1, 1763, folio 14.

HUARD, PIERRE
Corporal. Arrived in Louisiana in 1749 on the Chimine. He is of the company of Montcharvaux. See the general roll of troops for June 1, 1760

HUARD, PIERRE
Arrived in Louisiana on the Infante Victoire in 1751, company of Neyon. See the general roll of all the troops for the same day, June 1, 1760. Died at the hospital September 30, 1759. See the roll of June 1, 1760, folio 6. August 22, 1762, delivered his death certificate to Monsieur Huart of Senneville, his father, lieutenant of the company of bas officiers of the Invalides at Vincennes. The certificate is dated August 22, 1762.

HUARD, PIERRE
He is the third Pierre Huard on the general roll of troops for June 1, 1760. He is of the company of Reggio and was engaged December 3, 1756.

HUART, PIERRE
Engaged in 1756. Discharged November 30, 1768, roll of January 1, 1763, folio 36.

HUBE, ETIENNE

HUBERT, FRANCOIS
Discharged June 1, 1751.

HUBERT, JACQUES
Discharged November 30, 1769, roll of January 1, 1763, folio 43.

HUCHETTE, JEAN BAPTISTE NICOLAS
Died October 6, 1734. Death certificate in proper form at the Bureau des Invalides.

HUDAIN, ANTOINE JOSEPH
Discharged September 5, 1763, roll of January 1, 1763, folio 14.

HUILLEAU
Died November 5, 1738. Death certificate in proper form at the Bureau des Invalides.

HUISSON, CHARLES
Deserted the latter part of June, 1750.

HULLIR, RENÉ
Died November 4, 1738, at Akancas dans blanc.

HUNAUD, PIERRE
Deserted April 20, 1761. See the roll of the same year, folio 16.

HURTEBISE, GUILLAUME
Died at the hospital September 19, 1757, company of Sommes.

HUSSON, CLAUDE
Died May 20, 1750.

HUSSON, GASPARD
Discharged September 15, 1763, roll of January 1, 1763, folio 13.

LOUISIANA TROOPS —:— 1720-1770

IMBELLE, JEAN
  Discharged May 31, 1756.

LOUISIANA TROOPS —:— 1720-1770

JABLY, LAURENT
Extended leave and went to France on the royal vessel La Fortune January 1, 1759. See the roll of June 1, 1760, folio 12.

JACOB, JEAN BAPTISTE
Executed by the firing squad February 6, 1754, company of Pontalba.

JACOB, NICOLAS
Discharged July 29, 1756, company of Benoist.

JACQUELIN, MICHEL
Discharged November 30, 1769, roll of January 1, 1763, folio 47.

JACQUEMARD, JEAN

JACQUEMIN, JEAN BAPTISTSE

JACQUES
Negro servant of Monsieur Aubry. Drowned in the sinking of the Pere de Famille February 17, 1770, returning to France.

JACQUES, FRANCOIS
Discharged September 15, 1763, roll of January 1, 1763, folio 18.

JACQUES, JEAN
Drowned in the sinking of the Pere de Famille February 17, 1770, returning to France.

JACQUES, JEAN BAPTISTE
Discharged September 15, 1763, roll of January 1, 1763, folio 5.

JAGNAU, PIERRE
Discharged September 15, 1763, roll of January 1, 1763, folio 9.

JAMET, SIMON

JAMIN, JEAN BAPTISTE
Discharged August 20, 1770, with half-pay of 12 livres 10 sols per month according to a decision of October 17, 1770.

JAMIN, PHILIPPES
Deserted at New Orleans January 26, 1761. See the roll of the same year, folio 40.

JAMIER, PIERRE
Died at Fort Chartres April 30, 1755, company of Villiers.

JANNIAU, PIERRE
Fifer. With half-pay of 6 livres from April 4, 1764, sent to the Bureau des Invalides.

JAQUET, CHARLES
Engaged in 1768. Deserted September 10, 1769.

JAQUIN, JEAN
Discharged and went to France on the Rhinoceros July 10, 1754.

JARDELAS, ALLAIN
Discharged October 1, 1750.

JARDINS, PIERRE MAURICE
Deserted October 14, 1765. Condemned by contumacy following the judgement rendered in Louisiana October 17, 1765. Company of Trudeau.

JARRE, JEAN FRANCOIS
Deserted October 30, 1766, roll of January 1, 1763, folio 33

JATIERE, ETIENNE JEAN
Died October 1, 1751.

JEAN, JACQUES
Dismissed September 30, 1769, roll of January 1, 1763, folio 55.

JEAN, JEAN ANTOINE
Deserted November 20, 1756.

JEAN, PIERRE JOSEPH
Died at Mobile September 23, 1754, company of Grandmaison.

JOLIVET, FRANCOIS
Deserted February 5, 1739.

JOLIVET, LOUIS
Died November 9, 1751.

JOLIVET, THOMAS
Discharged September 15, 1763, roll of January 1, 1763, folio 6.

JOSSARD, FRANCOIS

JOSSE, ANTOINE
Discharged September 15, 1763, roll of January 1, 1763, folio 6.

JOSSEUX, JEAN BAPTISTE
  Discharged September 15, 17-63, roll of January 1, 1763, folio 6.

JOUBERT, PIERRE

JOUETTE, LOUIS
  Died May 14, 1751.

JOUGLAS, BARTHELEMY
  Deserted March 12, 1751.

JOUSSIANNE, PIERRE

JOURDAN, GUILLEAUME
  Died July 4, 1751.

JOURDAIN, EDME

JOURDAIN, JACQUES
  Died August 6, 1744, company of Marest.

JOURDAIN, JOSEPH
  Discharged September 15, 17-63, roll of January 1, 1763.

JOURDAIN, NICOLAS
  Discharged September 15, 17-63, roll of January 1, 1768, folio 10.

JOURDAIN, NICOLAS
  Discharged March 10, 1756. He re-enlisted.

JOUVENAY, FRANCOIS
  September 17, 1761, dispatched the death certificate to Monsieur Jacques Poupardis, royal officer. Drowned in the river February 12, 1754, company of Grandchamp.

JOUVENEL, BARTHELEMY
  Discharged April 18, 1756, went to France.

JOUX, DENIS
  Discharged September 15, 17-63, roll of January 1, 1763, folio 25.

JUILLET, MICHEL
  Discharged February 6, 1770, with half-pay of 12 livres per month according to a decision of April 28, 1770. Sergeant.

JULIE, RENÉ

JULIE, RENÉ
  Discharged August 10, 1754.

JULIEN, ROCH
  Discharged April 18, 1756.

JUPIN, JEAN BAPTISTE
  Discharged September 15, 17-63, roll of January 1, 1763, folio 22.

KEL, JACQUES

KEMER, MICHEL
Condemned by contumacy for desertion. See the proceedings of September 30, 1753.

KENIK, JEAN
Died January 11, 1751.

KERNER, ANTOIREK
Discharged August 1, 1768.

See the "Q" section.

KESTRE, GEORGE

KOLB, HENRY

KREMER, FREDERICK
Corporal of the Swiss regiment of Halwyl. With half-pay of 12 livres per month according to a decision of October 25, 1769, sent to the Bureau des Invalides October 27, 1769.

LA BARRE, JOSEPH
Cadet soldat. Died September 5, 1750, company of Monchervaux.

LABATTE, JACQUES
Discharged September 15, 1763, roll of January 1, 1763, folio 14.

LABAU, CHARLES

LABBÉ, PIERRE

LABORIE, GUILLEAUME
Discharged November 30, 1769, roll of January 1, 1763, folio 39.

LABORY, JEAN
Deserted July 27, 1759, and executed by the firing squad September 13, 1759. See the roll of June 1, 1760, folio 1.

LA BOULAYE, MATHURIN

LA BOULAYE, MATHURIN

LA BROSSE, NICOLAS
Discharged August 20, 1770, with half-pay of 6 livres per month according to a decision of November 2, 1770.

LA BRUYERE, BLAIZE
Died November 26, 1751.*

LA CARIE, FRANCOIS
Discharged September 15, 1763. Died at the hospital of Niort November 26, 1764,... death certificate delivered by the chaplain of the said hospital.

LA CAZE, ANTOINE

LA CAZE, JACQUES
Discharged May 1, 1750.

LACAZE, PIERRE

LA CHAISE, FRANCOIS
Died at New Orleans January 4, 1757, company of Grandpre.*

LA COMBE, ETIENNE
Soldier discharged from the Canadian troops with half-pay of 8 livres 2 sols. With half-pay of 2 livres per month according to a decision of September 22, 1763, sent to the Bureau des Invalides September 23, 1763.

LA CONTAINE, JOSEPH
Discharged September 15, 1763, roll of January 1, 1763, folio 25.

LACOU, JEAN
Sergeant, with half-pay of 16 livres per month according to a decision of April 4, 1764, sent to the Bureau des Invalides April 5, 1764. Discharged September 15, 1763.

LA COU, JEAN JOSEPH
Soldier on half-pay. Died on board the Thetis returning to France June 4, 1770. The death certificate is on file in Louisiana.

LACOU, PAUL

LACOUR, JACQUES
Died at the hospital August 23, 1756, company of Chabert.

LA COUR, PIERRE
Discharged at Natchitoches in 1768, roll of January 1, 1763, folio 36.

LA COURT, PIERRE

LA COUTURE, ARNOULT
Discharged June 1, 1751.

LA CROIX, PIERRE
Discharged September 15, 1763, roll of January 1, 1763, folio 21.

LADURANTÉE, JEAN
Died October 30, 1757, company of Pontalba.

LAFARGUE, JEAN

LA FLEUR, JACQUES
Discharged September 15, 1763, roll of January 1, 1763, folio 9

LA FLEUR, JEAN BAPTISTE
With half-pay of 6 livres per month according to a decision of June 11, 1764, sent to the Bureau des Invalides June 12, 1764.

LA FLEUR, PIERRE ANDRÉ
Discharged September 15, 1763, roll of January 1, 1763, folio 7.

LAFORGE, FRANCOIS
Deserted September 22, 1769, roll of January 1, 1763, folio 51.

LOUISIANA TROOPS —:— 1720-1770

LA FONTAINE, CLAUDE
Died June 14, 1750.
LA FOSSE, JACQUES
LA FOREST, CLAUDE
Discharged September 15, 17-63, roll of January 1, 1763, folio 8.
LA GARDE, BERNARD
Died March 7, 1751.
LAGE, JEAN AMAND
Died at the hospital January 11, 1758. See the roll of June 1, 1760, folio 8.
LA GLENE, JACQUES
Deserted July 4, 1756.
LA GOUTTE, JEAN
With half-pay of 6 livres per month since April 1, 1764. Discharged September 15, 1763, roll of January 1, 1763, folio 5. An additional allowance of 6 livres per month according to a decision of April 30, 1772.
LA GRANGE, HENRY
LA GRANGE, JEAN
With half-pay of 4 livres 10 sols per month according to a decision of June 11, 1764, sent to the Bureau des Invalides June 12, 1764. Discharged September 15, 1763, roll of January 1, 1763, folio 70.
LA GRANGE, LOUIS
LA HAYE, FRANCOIS LAURENT DE
Died at Illinois January 15, 1754, company of Monberberault.
LA HAYE, JACQUES
Discharged July 16, 1756. Went to France.
LA HAYE, JACQUES
LAHURE, NICOLAS
Discharged August 1, 1766, roll of January 1, 1763, folio 34.
LAIGLE, NICOLAS
Discharged February 6, 1770, company of Trudeau.
LAINÉ, JEAN CHARLES
LA LAGE, PIERRE
Discharged September 30, 17-69, roll of January 1, 1763, folio 35.

LA LANNE, JEAN
LALAINE, JEAN
LALEMAND, JOSEPH
Condemned to the gallies May 6, 1751.
LALLEMAND, JOSEPH
Discharged September 15, 17-63, roll of January 1,1763, folio 21.
LALOUETTE, JACQUES
LAOUETTE, JACQUES
Discharged July 10, 1754, and went to France on the vessel Rhinoceros
La MARFINIERE, JEAN BAPTISTE
LA MARQUE, PIERRE
Died December 18, 1751.
LA MARRE, JEAN FRANCOIS
Discharged July 1, 1750.
LAMARRE, PIERRE
LAMBERT, JEAN BAPTISTE
With half-pay of 4 lires 10 sols per month according to a decision of June 11, 1764, sent to the Bureau des Invalides June 12, 1764.
LAMBERT, JEAN LOUIS
Extended leave July 8, 1758. See the roll of June 1, 1760, folio 5.
LAMBERT, PIERRE JOSEPH
Discharged June 1, 1765, roll of January 1, 1763, folio 31.
LAMBERT, NICOLAS
LAMENDE or LAMANTE, JOSEPH FRANCOIS
Discharged September 15, 17-63, roll of January 1, 1763, folio 17.
LA MOTTE, JEAN FRANCOIS
Died at the hospital June 11, 1754, company of Du Tillet.
LAMARRE, PIERRE
With half-pay of 9 livres per month according to a decision of June 11, 1764, sent to the Bureau des Invalides June 12, 1764. Discharged September 15, 1763.
LAMY, JACQUES
LAMY, JACQUES
Died October 27, 1769, roll of January 1, 1763, folio 39.

LAMY, JACQUES
With half-pay of 9 livres per month according to a decision of April 4, 1764, sent to the Bureau des Invalides April 5, 1764. Sergeant. Discharged September 15, 1763. Drowned in the sinking of the Pere de Famille February 17, 1770, returning to France.

LANCELOT, BERNARD
Taken (prisoner) on the Fortune returning to Louisiana in 1756. Taken to England and returned May 1, 1763, with a passport of the same date and delivered in Boulogne where it was visaed at the bureau May 30, 1763, to be permanently discharged.

LANCELOT, LOUIS

LANCELOT, LOUIS
Discharged February 6, 1770, company of La Periere.

LANCIEN, JEAN
Licensed at Havre in February, 1761. See the general license roll made at that port from February 22, 1761, folio 5. With half-pay of 6 livres per month given on October 22, 1772.

LANON, PIERRE
Habitant since January 2, 1751.

LANDEZ, JEAN
Discharged April 18, 1756. Went to France

LANDROBY, JOSEPH
Invalid. Remained at Akancas from December 1, 1769, roll of January 1, 1763, folio 52.

LANDRY, JEAN BAPTISTE SIMON

LANE, PIERRE
Deserted September 27, 1756.

LA NEUVILLE, THOMAS
Died March 12, 1751.

LANGERONT, ETIENNE
Deserted April 15, 1755.

LANGLOIS, FRANCOIS
Discharged November 30, 1769, roll of January 1, 1763, folio 45.

LANGLOIS, JACQUES
Discharged June 1, 1751.

LANGLOIS, JEAN BAPTISTE
Deserted June 24, 1757 at Vera Cruz. See the roll of June 1, 1761, folio 10.

LANGLOIS, PIERRE
Died at New Orleans December 10, 1757, company of Grandchamp.

LANNIER, MARTIN
Deserted September 30, 1738, company of Le Blanc.

LA PARA, GUILLAUME
Discharged September 15, 1763, roll of January 1, 1763, folio 1.

LA PERINE, PIERRE
Discharged November 30, 1769, roll of January 1, 1763, folio 49.

LA PIERRE ANTOINE
Canonier bombadier. Discharged October 8, 1769 Drowned in the sinking of the Pere de Famille, February 17, 1770, returning to France.

LA PIERRE, FRANCOIS
With half-pay of 6 livres per month according to a decision of April 4, 1764, sent to the Bureau des Invalides April 5, 1764. Discharged September 15, 1763, roll of January 1, 1763, folio 10.

LA PLUYE, PIERRE
Died September 25, 1751.

LA PORTE, ANDRE
Remained at Arcankas from November 31, 1769, roll of January 1, 1763, folio 51.

LAPORTE, FRANCOIS
Discharged August 1, 1765, roll of January 1, 1763, folio 31.

LA PORTE, JEAN
Discharged August 31, 1756, company of Derneville.

LAPORTE, JOSEPH
Discharged September 15, 1763, roll of January 1, 1763, folio 17

LA POULE, CLAUDE FRANCOIS
Discharged November 16, 1769, roll of January 1 1763, folio 46.

LARDAT, JEAN
Discharged June 1, 1756.

LARDIN, JACQUES

LA RENAUDIERE CHARLES
Discharged February 1, 1757.

LA RIBARDIERE, CHARLES
Discharged February 1, 1751.

LA RIBADIERE, CHARLES
With half-pay of 6 livres per month payable at Paris, served since 1720, presented his discharge delivered at New Orleans March 12, 1768. In the margin of his discharge is written: "Served in this colony since 1720 and obtained half-pay of 6 livres per month in 1751, by order of the court."

LA RIVIERE, CHARLES
Died January 20, 1750.

LARMOND, PIERRE
Discharged October 31, 1769, roll of January 1, 1763, folio 43.

LA ROCHE, JACQUES
Discharged September 15, 1763, roll of January 1, 1768, folio 22.

LA ROCHE, JACQUES
Died October 23, 1737.

LA ROCHELLE, SIMON

LA RONCE, FRANCOIS GILLES GERME.
Discharged September 15, 1763, roll of January 1, 1768 folio 14.

LAROQUETTE, JEAN
Deserted October 14, 1765. Condemned by contumacy following the judgement rendered in Louisiana October 17, 1765. Company of Villiers.

LA ROSE, BENOIST
Discharged September 15, 1763, roll of January 1, 1768, folio 23.

LAROZE, BENOIT
With half-pay of 9 livres per month according to a decision of April 4, 1764, sent to the Bureau des Invalides.

LA ROZIERE, GUILLAUME BERNARD
Discharged February 6, 1770, with half-pay of 4 livres, 10 sols per month according to a decision of April 28, 1770.

LARRIERE, NICOLAS

LARRIERE, NICOLAS
With half-pay of 16 livres per month according to a decision of April 4, 1764, sent to the Bureau des Invalides April 5, 1764.

LA SAIGNE, LEONARD
Discharged September 1, 1751.

LA SALLE, FRANCOIS
Deserted December 26, 1767, roll of January 1, 1763, folio 34.

LA SEIGNE, LEONARD
Discharged October 1, 1754.

LASSAIGNE, CLAUDE
Died at the hospital April 10, 1754, company of Macarty.

LATTIER, JOSEPH

LAUBEL, JEAN BAPTISTE

LAUBIERE, PIERRE

LAUNAY, CHARLES
Died at Natchitoches January 19, 1765, roll of January 1, 1763, folio 31.

LAURENSCON, JEAN

LAURENDINE, PIERRE
Discharged September 15, 1763, roll of January 1, 1763, folio 4.

LAURENT, CLAUDE
Discharged September 15 1763, roll of January 1, 1763, folio 24.

LAURENT, JACQUES

LAURENT, LOUIS
Discharged September 15, 1763, roll of January 1, 1763, folio 8.

LAVAL, PIERRE
Deserted at Vera Cruz July 11, 1757. See the roll of June 1, 1760, folio 4.

LAVAL, PIERRE
Deserted July 11, 1757.

LAVAL, SEBASTIEN
Discharged February 6, 1770, with half-pay of 15 livres per month, according to a decision of April 28, 1770. Died at the hospital at La Rochelle February 2, 1770 (sic.) The death certificate attached to M. Le Moyne's letter was placed with the rolls of the Isle of Re for the month of July, 1770.

LA VALLÉE, JEAN
Died October 15, 1737.

LA VALLE, SEBASTIEN

LA VANNERIE, ANTOINE
Deserted September 1, 1754.

LAVIS, JACQUES
Discharged October 1, 1750.

LAVAU, ANTOINE

LAYETE, NICOLAS
Went to France on the Samson October 4, 1769, roll of January 1, 1763, folio 54.

LA VERTU, LOUIS

LA VIGNE, PIERRE
Died at Mobile (date blank).

LA VILLE, ANTOINE

LA VILLE, JEAN

LA VILLE, PIERRE
Discharged September 15, 1763, roll of January 1, 1763, folio 4.

LA VILLE, THOMAS

LA VOIZE, NICOLAS
Discharged September 15, 1763, roll of January 1, 1763, folio 16.

LEBAS, JOSEPH ROBERT
Died descending from Illinois December 15, 1775, company of Monchervaux.

LE BLANC, ANTOINE
Executed by the firing squad February 9, 1756, company of Monchervaux.

LEBLANC CHARLES
Discharged September 15, 1763, roll of January 1, 1763, folio 2.

LE BLANC, GUILLEAUME
Died at Tombekbe January 14, 1754, company of Villemont.

LEBLANC, JEAN
Died at Illinois December 15, 1745, company of Le Verrier.

LE BLANC, PAUL GUILLAUME
Died November 4, 1751.

LE BLOND, PIERRE

LE BLOND, PIERRE
Drowned in the sinking of the Pere de Famille February 17, 1770, returning to France.

LE BOUCHÉ, RENÉ
Discharged September 15, 1763, roll of January 1, 1763, folio 1.

LE BOULANGER, FRANCOIS
Died June 26, 1736.

LEBRETON, ANTOINE
Died December 25, 1745, company of Benoist.

LEBRUN, CLAUDE
Died October 1, 1751.

LE BRUN, JACQUES

LE BRUN, JACQUES

LE CAU, MATHURIN
Discharged September 15, 1763, roll of January 1, 1763, folio 16.

LE CLERC, JEAN BAPTISTE
Died at the Balize August 1, 1746, (regiment of?) Gavorit.

LE CLERC, PATRICE

L'ECLUSE, JACQUES FRANCOIS JOSEPH DE
Discharged \April 18, 1756, went to France.

LE COEUR, GABRIEL
Deserted October 14, 1765. Condemned by contumacy Following the judgement rendered in Louisiana October 17, 1765. Company of Trudeau.

LE COINTRE, ETIENNE
Discharged September 15, 1763, roll of January 1, 1763, folio 19.

LE COINTRE, JEAN FRANCOIS

LE COMTE, CHARLES
Drowned in Illinois July 7, 1755, company of Chabert.

LE COMTE, CLEMENT
Died March 9, 1746, sergeant in the company of Orgon.

LOUISIANA TROOPS —:— 1720-1770

LE COMTE, FRANCOIS
Executed by the firing squad April 6, 1757, company of Grandpre.

LE COMTE, JEAN BAPTISTE

LE COMTE, JEAN BAPTISTE
Discharged September 15, 1763, roll of January 1, 1763, folio 19.

LE COMTE, JEAN ETIENNE

LE COMTE, JOSEPH
Died at the hospital March 10, 1767, roll of January 1, 1763, folio 34.

LECOMTE, LOUIS
Discharged February 6, 1770, with half-pay of 9 livres per month according to a decision of April 28, 1770.

LE COMTE, LOUIS
Died December 26, 1751.

LE COMTE, LOUIS
Died March 27, 1738.

LE COQ, GEORGES
Deserted June 27, (1758), arrested July 7, (1758), condemned to be executed by the firing squad July 23, 1758. See the roll June 1, 1760., folio 3.

LE COURDONNIER, CHARLES FRANCOS
Discharged. See the roll dated at Calais May 2, 1763.

LE COURT, JACQUES
With half-pay of 6 livres per month according to a decision of April 4, 1764, sent to the Bureau des Invalides April 5, 1764.

LE CUIT, PERRE
Died April 28, 1734.

LE CURON, GUILLEAUME
Discharged September 15, 1763, roll of January 1, 1763, folio 6.

L'ECUYER, ETIENNE

L'ECUYER, ETIENNE
Discharged January 2, 1766, roll of January 1, 1763, folio 32.

LEFEBVRE, RENÉ
Died April 10, 1745, company of Gauvry.

LEFEVRE, ANTOINE
Died at Mobile February 21, 1754, company of Bonnille.

LEFEVRE, JEAN
Dishcarged May 21, 1756.

LE FEVRE, JOSEPH

LE FEVRE, NICOLAS

LEFEVRE, NICOLAS MARTIN

LEFEVRE, NICOLAS
Deserted at Pointe Coupee December 17, 1758, company of Chavoye. See the general roll of June 1, 1760, folio 10. Discharged September 15, 1763.

LEFEVRE, RODOLPHE
Died January 27, 1739, company of La Buissonniere.

LEFEVRE, SIMON CLAUDE

L'EFF, HENRY
Discharged September 15, 1763, roll of January 1, 1763, folio 16.

LE FLOT, JEAN BAPTISTE

LE FORT, JEAN
Died September 6, 1751.

LEFORT, JEAN ANTOINE
Drowned in Bayou St. Jean June 23, 1765, roll of January 1, 1763, folio 31.

LEFORT, PIERRE
Discharged July 1, 1750.

LEGAI, JEAN GABRIEL
Sergeant. Discharged February 6, 1770, with half-pay of 12 livres per month according to a decision of April 28, 1770.

LEGAL, HENRY LOUSI
Died November 1, 1737.

LEGAL, THOMAS
Died May 8, 1738.

LEGARNIER, PIERRE
Drowned March 14, 1751.

LE GAUD, MATHIEU
Habitant since February 12, 1753.

LE GAUFFRE, PIERRE
Discharged September 15, 1763, roll of January 1, 1763, folio 21.

LOUISIANA TROOPS —:— 1720-1770

LEGER, CHARLES
Discharged September 15, 1763, with half-pay of 4 livres 10 sols per month according to a decision of April 4, 1764, sent to the Bureau des Invalides April 5, 1764.

LE GRAIN, LOUIS PIERRE
Died April 6, 1746. Sergeant in the company of Blanc.

LE GRAND, JACQUES
Discharged October 1, 1751.

LE GRAND, JEAN
Discharged May 21, 1761, being unworthy of serving the King in any respect. See the roll of the same year, folio 32.

LE GRAND, JEAN BAPTISTE
Discharged October 1, 1769, roll of January 1, 1763, folio 47.

LE GRAND, CHARLES
Deserted June 4, 1756.

LEGRAND, PIERRE
Discharged August 1, 1765, roll of January 1, 1763, folio 32.

LE GRAND, PIERRE
Corporal. With half-pay of 12 livres per month according to a decision of November 19, 1765, sent to the Bureau des Invalides November 20, 1765.

LE GUAY, JEAN GABRIEL

LE GUÉ, RENÉ
Discharged September 15, 1763, roll of January 1, 1763, folio 26.

LEGUENEE (?), GUILLAUME

LE GUERNÉ, PIERRE

LE HÉRANT, JACQUES
Discharged October 31, 1769, roll of January 1, 1763, folio 47.

LEHUT, JEAN

LE JEUNE, PIERRE
Died May 29, 1735.

LE LEU, LOUIS
Habitant since May 1, 1752.

LE LONG, BARTHELEMY
Discharged September 15, 1763, roll of January 1, 1763, folio 19.

LE MAIRE, PHILIP JOSEPH
Died at the hospital February 9, 1759. See the roll of June 1, 1760, folio 11.

LE MAITRE, JEAN
Drowned in Illinois June 25, 1757. See the roll of June 1, 1759, folio 8.

LE MAITRE, JEAN
Drowned at Illinois June 25, 1757, company of Gourdon.

LE MASLE, JEAN
Died, company of Grandpre. The date of his death is not on the roll.

LE MASSON, MATHURIN

LE MAURE, MICHEL
Died at the hospital February 7, 1759. See the roll of June 1, 1760, folio 6.

LEMELE, ANDRÉ

LE MESLE, ANDRÉ
Died at the hospital March 11, 1759. See the roll of June 1, 1760, folio 9.

LE MINEUR, LOUIS
Discharged July 23, 1751.

LE MOYNE, FRANCOIS
Died January 4, 1737.

LE MOYNE, JEAN

LE NEZ, FRANCOIS
With half-pay of 4 livres 10 sols per month according to a decision of October 10, 1764, sent to the Bureau des Invalides the same day. Discharged June 1, 1764.

LENEZ, JEAN
Drowned in the river January 10, 1754, company of Aubry.

LEON, GASPART
Died at Natchitoches March 31, 1769, roll of January 1, 1763, folio 47.

LE PRESTRE, JACQUES
Died December 10, 1751.

LEQUARRE, JEAN
Went to France on the Pere de Famille November 24, 1769, roll of January 1, 1763, folio 37

LOUISIANA TROOPS —:— 1720-1770

LEQUERCE or LE THIERS FRANCOIS
See the list of M de Repentigny for February 6, 1770

LE RAT, PIERRE GEORGES
Deserted at Arkancas October 26, 1759. See the roll of June 1, 1760, folio 2.

LE RAT, PIERRE GEORGES
Deserted at Arkancas October 26, 1759. See the roll of June 1, 1760, folio 2.

LE ROY, DENIS
Discharged July 1, 1750.

LE ROY ETIENNE

LESCOMBE, JOSEPH ANDRÉ

LESCOUYER, THOMAS

LESTANG, JEAN
Discharged September 15, 1763, roll of January 1, 1763, folio 4.

L'ETERNEL, NOEL

LE TEURS, GUILLEAUME
Corporal. Discharged September 15, 1763. With half-pay of 9 livres per month according to a decision of April 4, 1764, sent to the Bureau des Invalides April 5, 1764, payable at Rouen.

LE TEVET, ANTOINE
Drowned in the river October 17, 1755, company of Aubry.

LE TIER, FRANCOIS
See Thiers in the "T" section. Discharged September 15, 1763, roll of January 1, 1763, folio 20.

LE TUEUR, GUILLAUME

LE TURC, JEAN BAPTISTE
Died at the hospital January 20, 1767, roll of January 1, 1763, folio 34.

LEURASGUE, PAUL ANTOINE
Discharged June 21, 1756.

LE VACHER, EDMÉ FRANCOIS
Died August 15, 1745, company of Gauvry.

LE VASSEUR, JEAN
Died May 6, 1738.

LE VEGUE, FRANCOIS

LEVREAU, JEROSME

LEXCELLENT, CHARLES
Corporal. With half-pay of 9 livres per month according to a decision of April 4, 1764, sent to the Bureau des Invalides April 5, 1764.

LEXCELLENT, CHARLES
Corporal. Discharged September 10, 1763, after serving served 26 years, half-pay of 9 livres per month of which he asks to be paid at Chatillon sur Seine in Bourgogne.

LEYNE, JEAN
Engaged in 1764. Discharged September 30, 1769, roll of January 1, 1763, folio 54.

LEYSTER, THOMAS

LHERMAND, PERRE
Discharged July 16, 1754.

L' HIVER, PIERRE
Discharged September 15, 1763, roll of January 1, 1763, folio 7.

LHOMMEAU, JEAN BAPTISTE
Drowned descending from Natchez October 2, 1754, company of Mazan.

LHOMME, CLAUDE

LHOMME, CLAUDE
Discharged February 6, 1770, with half-pay of 6 livres per month, according to a decision of April 28, 1770.

LHOMMON, JEAN
Discharged July 10, 1756. Went to France.

LHORMAND, PIERRE
Discharged July 16, 1754. Went to France.

LHUILLIER, JOSEPH

LIBSTER, JEAN
Discharged September 31, 1763, after having served 264 months with half-pay of 12 livres per month, and asks to (be payed) in Alsace. Corporal of the Swiss Regiment of Hallwyck.

LIGERBOULT, FREDERIC
Died at the Tonikas August 4, 1757, company of Gamont.

LINERALE, BLAISE
Died October 22, 1738.

LOBEL, JEAN
LOGIS, NICOLAS
LOGIS, NICOLAS
LOISEAU, FRANCOIS
   Died at the Vincennes Post March 31, 1757, company of Hazeur.
LOISON, MICHEL
   Died at the hospital September 18, 1754, company of Grandchamp.
LONGUAY, PIERRE
   With half-pay of 8 livres per month, according to a decision of November 19, 1765, sent to the Bureau des Invalides November 20, 1765. Discharged September 15, 1763, roll of January 1, 1763, folio 2.
LONGUEMARE, FRANCOIS
LOQUIES, ANTOINE
LOQUIN, ANTOINE
   Deserted September 18, 1756.
LOREA, JEROSME
   Died November 16, 1751.
LORETTE, CHARLES
   Deserted at Arkancas October 26, 1759. See the roll of June 1, 1760, folio 5.
LORIAU, MATHIEU
   Discharged August 20, 1770, with half-pay of 6 livres per month according to a decision of October 17, 1770.

LORINE, JACQUES
   Discharged September 15, 1763, roll of January 1, 1763, folio 1.
LORIOT, MATHEU
LOUINARD, FRANCOIS
LOUIS, HENRY
   Discharged November 30, 1769, roll of January 1, 1763, folio 47.
LOUIS, JEAN
   Half-pay of 4 livres 10 sols per month according to a decision of June 11, 1764, sent to the Bureau des Invalides June 12, 1764.
LOUMAR, FRANCOIS
   Discharged February 6, 1770, with half-pay of 4 livres 10 sols per month according to a decision of April 28, 1770.
LOUVIGNY, JACQUES
LOBEL, JEAN BAPTISTE
LUQUET, PIERRE
   Discharged September 15, 1763, roll of January 1, 1763, folio 25.
LUQUET, PIERRE
   With half-pay of 9 livres per month according to a decision of June 11, 1764, sent to the Bureau des Invalides the same day. Discharged September 15, 1763.
LUSSEAU, PIERRE
   Died at Illinois December 19, 1763, roll of January 1, 1763, folio 11.

LOUISIANA TROOPS —:— 1720-1770

MABIRE, JEAN
Died September 11, 1755, company of Montberault.

MACARD, JOSEPH

MACÉE, PIERRE
Deserted February 5, 1739.

MACON, HENRY
Deserted July 4, 1755.

MACROHON, CORNELIUS
Discharged November 30, 1768, roll of January 1, 1763, folio 36.

MACTEAU, JACQUES
Died January 10, 1757, company of d'Hauterive.

MADAL, JEAN
Discharged September 15, 1763, roll of January 1, 1763, folio 20.

MAFRE, CLAUDE

MAGNANAUT, VINCENT
Deserted in 1754.

MAGNY, JEAN
Drowned February 20, 1763, roll of January 1, 1763, folio 23.

MAGNY, NICOLAS
Discharged October 1, 1757.

MAIGROS, ANTOINE
Died at Natchitoches January 31, 1765, roll of January 1, 1763, folio 31.

MAIGROS, JACQUES
Discharged June 1 1750.

MAILLARD, JEAN
Died at the hospital January 13, 1755, company of Darazola.

MAILLARD, JEAN JACQUES
Discharged September 15, 1763, roll of January 1, 1763 folio 16.

MAILLARD, PIERRE

MAINARD, PIERRE

MAIRE, JEAN

MAIRE, JOSEPH

MAIRE, NICOLAS
Discharged September 15, 1763, roll of January 1, 1763, folio 3.

MAISONNEUVE, CHARLES
Died December 26, 1755, company of Artaud.

MAITRE, JOSEPH
Condemned by contumacy for desertion. See the criminal proceedings of September 30, 1753.

MALAGÉE, JEAN

MALBERT, JEAN BAPTISTE
Discharged Septemebr 15, 1763, roll of January 1, 1763, folio 14.

MALICE, MICHEL
Discharged February 1, 1764, roll of January 1, 1763, folio 30.

MANARD, JEAN FRANCOIS
Died January 7, 1737.

MANASSA, JEAN BAPTISTE

MANATA, JEAN BAPTISTE

MANCELLE, ALEXIS
Discharged at Calais October 13, 1762. See the roll of the same day. With half-pay of 8 livres per month according to a decision of April 15, 1767.

MANCIAU, DENIS
Went to France on the Samson October 1, 1769, roll of January 1, 1763, folio 50.

MANDOXA, FELIX
Discharged July 1, 1764, roll of January 1, 1763, folio 28.

MANDRÉ, HENRY

MANELLE, JACQUES
Died at the hospital September 6, 1757, company of Villiers.

MANG, CHRISTIAN
Discharged January 31, 1764, after having served 3 3 0 months. Corporal, Hallwyl's Swiss Regiment. Half-pay of 12 livres per month, asking to be paid in Alsace.

MANGIN, DENIS
Company of Villiers. Discharged February 6, 1770.

MANJARD or MANGEARD, NICOLAS
Discharged September 15, 1763, roll of January 1, 1763, folio 10.

MANJEAU, DENIS

LOUISIANA TROOPS —:— 1720-1770

MANICLAIR, JACQUES LOUIS
With half-pay of 6 livres per month according to a decision of March 22, 1765, sent to the Bureau des Invalides. Discharged September 15, 1763, roll of January 1, 1763, folio 26.

MANIME, JEAN BAPTISTE
Discharged June 1, 1751.

MANNEQUIN, ANDRÉ

MANOT, ALEXIS

MANSARD, PIERRE
Died at the hospital January 10, 1756, company of La Houssaye.

MANSECOURT, JEAN
Died at Illinois January 18, 1755, company of La Houssaye.

MANTEL, JEAN

MANTEL, PIERRE

MANTER, JEAN PIERRE
Discharged September 15, 1763, roll of January 1, 1763, folio 17.

MAQUIGNON, CLAUDE
Died at Illinois December 15, 1745, company of Macarty.

MARAIS, NICOLAS
Discharged September 15, 1763 roll of January 1, 1763, folio 12.

MARC
Irishman. Servant of Monsieur La Forest de Maumont, Lieutenant of the Infantry. Drowned in the sinking of the Pere de Famille February 17, 1770, returning to France.

MARC, FRANCOIS

MARC, FRANCOIS
Died November 4, 1751.

MARCANTEL, FRANCOIS
Discharged October 30, 1756.

MARCELLE, JEAN
Drummer, company of Benoist. Discharged October 1, 1764, roll of January 1, 1763, folio 28.

MARCHAND, BERNARD
Discharged March 1, 1765, roll of January 1, 1763, folio 31.

MARCHAND, FRANCOIS
Died January 26, 1746, company of Marest.

MARCHAND, FRANCOIS
Died December 26, 1736.

MARCHAND, JEAN NICOLAS
Discharged September 15, 1763, roll of January 1, 1763, folio 2.

MARCHAND, LOUIS
Discharged October 8, 1769, roll of January 1, 1763, folio 49.

MARCHAND, PIERRE

MARCHE, JEAN
Discharged September 15, 1763, roll of January 1, 1763, folio 7

MARCOU, GUILLEAUME

MARESCHAL, CLAUDE

MARECHAL, CLAUDE
Discharged July 16, 1754, went to France.

MARECHAL, JEAN
Discharged September 30, 1769, roll of January 1, 1763, folio 53.

MARETTE, NICOLAS
Discharged March 1, 1751.

MARGOTTA, JACQUES
With half-pay of 6 livres per month according to a decision of June 11, 1764, sent to the Bureau des Invalides June 12, 1764.

MARIÉ, ALEXIS
Discharged September 15, 1763, roll of January 1, 1763, folio 7.

MARIÉ, JEAN BAPTISTE
Died July 20, 1751.

MARLIER, CHARLES
Discharged May 31, 1761. See the roll of the same year, folio 5.

MARMILLON, JACQUES DANIEL
Deserted December 12, 1745, at Natchitoches.

MARMOTTE, PELLERIN
Drowned September 3, 1750.

MARQUET, JEAN BAPTISTE
Died June 25, 1751.

MARSANT, BERNARD
With half-pay of 6 livres per month according to a decision of June 24, 1765, sent to the Bureau des Invalides June 25, 1765.

MARQUIS, JOSEPH
Discharged October 16, 1769, roll of January 1, 1763, folio 45.

MARTENNE, CLAUDE
Extended leave, went to France on the Royal vessel La Fortune January 1, 1759. See the roll of June 1, 1760, folio 3.

MARTIER, PIERRE

MARTIN, FRANCOIS
Died July 25, 1751.

MARTIN, HELLAIRE
Died February 5, 1751.

MARTIN, HENRY
With half-pay of 8 livres per month according to a decision of September 22, 1765, sent to the Bureau des Invalides September 25, 1765.

MARTIN, JEAN

MARTIN, JEAN
Discharged February 6, 1770, with half-pay of 4 livres 10 sols per month according to a decision of April 28, 1770.

MARTIN, JEAN LOUIS

MARTIN, JEAN LOUIS
Discharged in Louisiana November 30, 1768, presented to the Bureau and received half-pay of 6 livres per month according to a decision of June 18, 1769, sent to the Bureau des Invalides.

MARTIN, NICOLAS
Discharged September 15, 1763, roll of January 1, 1763, folio 7.

MARTIN, PIERRE
Discharged Septemebr 15, 1763, roll of January 1, 1763, folio 9.

MARTIN, PIERRE
Engaged April 1, 1769. Discharged October 8, 1769, roll of January 1, 1763, folio 39.

MARTIN, THOMAS
Executed by the firing squad August 11, 1751.

MARTRE or MARTHRE, JOSEPH
Deserted October 21, 1759. See the roll of June 1, 1760, folio 11.

MASSAN, BARTHELEMY
Discharged February 6, 1770, company of Mazilliere.

MASSÉ, GEORGES
Drowned while descending from Natchez October 2, 1754, company of Montberault.

MASSÉ, LOUIS

MASSENT, BARTHELEMI

MASSOLLE, LAURENT
Discharged September 15, 1763, roll of January 1, 1763, folio 14.

MASSON, FRANCOIS JOSEPH
With half-pay of 6 livres per month according to a decision of April 4, 1764, sent to the Bureau des Invalides April 5, 1764. Discharged September 15, 1763.

MASSON, GUILLEAUME
Died October 2, 1751.

MASSON, JULLIEN
Deserted July 17, 1755.

MASSY, PIERRE
Drowned while descending from Natchez October 2, 1754, company of Gamont.

MASTE, JEAN JACQUES
Died at the village of the Germans November 16, 1757, company of Hazeur.

MATAGRIN, ANDRÉ
Drowned April 17, 1764, roll of January 1, 1763, folio 28.

MATHIEU, FRANCOIS
Died December 6, 1750

MATHIEU, JOSEPH

MATHIEU, JOSEPH
Deserted May 14, 1758, company of Derneville.

MATHIEU, NICOLAS
Died December 8, 1745, company of de Blanc.

MAUCHATILLON, JEAN
Discharged May 1, 1757, to became habitant.

MAUGEIN, DENIS

MAUGEIN, SIMION
Drowned in the sinking of the Pere de Famille February 17, 1770, returning to France.

MAUGER, JEAN
Died at the hospital at New Orleans March 26, 1761. See the roll of the same year, folio 6.

MAUGIN, SIMON

MAUGNA, JOSEPH
Discharged Septemebr 15, 1763, roll of January 1, 1763, folio 18.

MAUREGAT, JEAN

MAURICE, PIERRE
With half-pay of 9 livres per month according to a decision of June 11, 1764, sent to the Bureau des Invalides June 12, 1764.

MAURICE, SIMON
With half-pay of 4 livres 10 sols per month according to a decision of June 11, 1764, sent to the Bureau des Invalides June 12, 1764.

MAURY, PIERRE
Died at the hospital February 3, 1756, company Des Mazelliers.

MAYER, NICOLAS

MAYNOT, CHARLES
Went to Santo Domingo July 22, 1763 on the frigate Aigrette, roll of January 1, 1763, folio 3.

MAZERO, JEAN
Died May 24 1738.

MAZURRE, PIERRE
Died January 1, 1756, company of Des Varennes.

MELIERS, PIERRE
Died July 21, 1736.

MEMIN, LOUIS
Sergeant. With half-pay of 12 livres per month according to a decision of April 4, 1764, sent to the Bureau des Invalides April 5, 1764. Discharged September 15, 1763.

MENAGE, LOUIS ETIENNE

MENAGER, JEAN
Dscharged September 15, 1763, roll of January 1, 1763, folio 23.

MENANT, PIERRE
With half-pay of 8 livres 10 sols per month according to a decision of August 22, 1764, sent to the Bureau des Invalides August 5, 1764.

MENARD, GILBERT
Died January 21, 1754, company of Villiers.

MENARD, GUILLEAUME
Died May 17, 1751.

MENELET, NICOLAS
Discharged June 12, 1754.

MENOU, JACQUES
Disharged April 1, 1756.

MERCIER, GILBERT
Deserted January 26, 1761. See the roll of the same year, folio 16.

MERCIER, JEAN
With half-pay of 6 livres per month according to a decision of April 4, 1764, sent to the Bureau des Invalides April 5, 1764. Discharged Septemebr 15, 1763.

MERCIER, PHILIPPES
Died at the hospital May 1, 1766, roll of January 1, 1763, folio 33.

MERCIER, PIERRE

MERCIER, PIERRE
Discharged February 6, 1770, company of Villiers.

MERCIER, RENE

MERICE, JEAN
With half-pay of 9 livres per month according to a decision of June 11, 1764, sent to the Bureau des Invalides June 12, 1764. Discharged Septemebr 15, 1763, roll of January 1, 1763, folio 9.

MERNOS, ANTOINE
Sergeant. Discharged in Louisiana November 20, 1769. Went to France on the Pere de Famille. With half-pay of 12 livres per month according to a decision of April 28, 1770.

MERVILLON, RENÉ
Deserted June 15, 1756.

MESNARD, GABRIEL
Deserted at Arkancas October 26, 1759. See the roll of June 1, 1760, folio 4.

MESSIN, NICOLAS ANTOINE
Died June 18, 1751.

METAILLES, JACQUES
Dsicharged September 15, 1763, roll of January 1, 1763, folio 23.

METAYER, JACQUES
Discharged September 30, 1769, roll of January 1, 1763, folio 51

METIVEL, JEAN BAPTISTE
Died at the hospital at Mobile December 6, 1754, company of Marentin.

METOYER, PIERRE
Died February 27 1764, roll of January 1, 1763, folio 29.

METZER, PHILIPPE
With half-pay of 12 livres 10 sols, per month according to a decision of April 4, 1764, sent to the Bureau des Invalides April 5, 1764. Licensed from the company of the canoniers bombardiers where he was corporal from September 15, 1763, by order of the King of March 3, 1764, supplementing his lost discharge papers sent the same day to Monsieur de Luce, intendant at Strasbourg.

METZGER, JEAN PHILIPPE
Discharged September 15, 1763, roll of January 1, 1763, folio 1.

MEUDRE, CLAUDE
Discharged at Calais with half-pay of 9 livres per month October 13, 1762. See the roll of the same day.

MEUNIER, LOUIS
Died October 26, 1751.

MEURE, ETIENNE
Extended leave and went to France on the royal vessel La Fortune January 1, 1759. See the roll of June 1, 1760, folio 7.

MEUSNIER, PIERRE
Discharged September 15, 1763, roll of January 1, 1763, folio 5.

MEZIERES, CLAUDE
Died at Mobile April 24, 1758. See the roll of June 1, 1760, folio 4.

MICHAUD, JACQUES
Died April 10, 1751.

MICHAUD, LOUIS
Discharged May 1, 1764, roll of January 1, 1763, folio 29.

MICHEL, LOUIS

MICHEL, LOUIS
Discharged April 18, 1756, went to France.

MIDON, CLAUDE

MIGNARDIN, JACQUES
Discharged July 16, 1756. Went to France.

MIGNOT, NICOLAS
Discarged June 1, 1764, roll of January 1, 1763, folio 28.

MIGNOT, PIERRE
Died at the hospital March 10, 1767, roll of January 1, 1763 folio 34.

MIKEL, MICHEL
Executed by the firing squad February 27, 1751.

MILLAN, CLAUDE
Discarged September 15, 1763, roll of January 1, 1763, folio 17.

MILLER, JEAN GEORGES
Discharged October 8, 1769, roll of January 1, 1763, folio 55.

MILLOT, CHARLES
Discharged December 1, 1764, roll of January 1, 1763, folio 26.

MILLOT, NICOLAS
With half-pay of 4 livres 10 sols according to a decision of March 22, 1765, sent to the Bureau des Invalides. Discharged March 1, 1765.

MILORY, JEAN
Died Septemebr 19, 1734.

MILSAN, JEAN FRANCOIS

MINIER,, FRANCOIS

LOUISIANA TROOPS —:— 1720-1770

MINQUE, GUILLEAUME
Died January 22, 1738.
MIODONET, JEAN
MIRANDOLE, PIERRE
Discharged September 15, 17-63, roll of January 1, 1763, folio 14.
MIREL, JOACHIM
Dismissed March 22, 1751.
MIROLD, JOSEPH ANTOINE
Discharged September 30, 17-69, roll of January 1, 1763, folio 42.
MISSONNIERE, JEAN BAPTISTE
Discharged February 1, 1764, roll of January 1, 1763, folio 26.
MISSUER, FRANCOIS
With half-pay of 6 livres per month according to a decision of April 4, 1764, sent to the Bureau des Invalides April 5, 1764.
MOLARD, CLAUDE
Died at the hospital January 9, 1755, company of Montberault.
MOLORET, EMMOND THOMAS..
Discharged March 1, 1750.
MONCHER, BARTHELEMY
Corporal. With half-pay of 9 livres per month according to a decision of April 4, 1764, sent to the Bureau des Invalides April 5, 1764. Discharged September 15, 1763.
MONDION, PIERRE
MONESTA, JEAN BAPTISTE
Discharged February 6, 1770, company of Duplessis.
MONET, MATHIEU
MONGENAY, JEAN
MONGET, JEAN MICHEL
MONHARD, PIERRE
Died at the hospital August 11, 1765, roll of January 1, 1763, folio 30.
MONJENET, JEAN
Company of Villiers. Discharged February 6, 1770.
MONIGET, JEAN
MONIOT, PIERRE
MONQUOIR, FRANCOIS

MONTARDY, PIERRE
Remained at Illinois, roll of January 1, 1763, folio 46.
MONTECHE, DOMINIQUE
Discharged April 1, 1750.
MONTEL, PIERRE
Soldier, company of Grandmaison. Discharged January 10, 1764, with half-pay of 9 livres per month according to a decision of October 27, 1769, sent to the Bureau des Invalides October 27, 1769.
MONTENOL, FRANCOIS
Died October 24, 1738.
MOQUIN, SIMON
Deserted August 1, 1758. See the roll of June 1, 1760, folio 11.
MORANDY, JEAN
Discharged September 1, 1751.
MORARE, FRANCOIS
Discharged September 15, 17-63, roll of January 1, 1763, folio 18.
MOREAU, ALEXANDRE
MOREAU, BIDAU VIDAL
Drowned at Ouabache November 10, 1756, company of Villiers.
MOREAU, JEAN BAPTISTE
Died September 18, 1761. See the roll of the year 1761, folio 24.
MOREAU, PAUL
Discharged July 1, 1750.
MOREAU, PIERRE
Deserted June 3, 1757.
MOREAU, PIERRE JEAN
Discharged August 31, 1763, roll of January 1, 1763, folio 12.
MOREAU, PIERRE
Discharged February 1, 1751.
MOREAU, THEODORE
Deserted January 21, 1738, company of La Buissonniere.
MOREL, ANDRÉ
Discharged August 1, 1755.

LOUISIANA TROOPS —:— 1720-1770

MOREL, JEAN
Sergeant, company of La Gautray. With half-pay of 12 livres per month according to a decision of November 30, 1764, sent to the Bureau des Invalides December 1, 1764. Discharged July 1, 1764.

MOREL, NICOLAS
Died September 17, 1751.

MORELLE, ANDRÉ
Discharged November 30, 1769, roll of January 1, 1763, folio 42.

MORGA, PIERRE
Discharged September 5 1763, roll of January 1, 1763, folio 25.

MORGAT, PIERRE

MORIN, MARC ANTOINE

MORIN, MARC ANTOINE
With his wife and daughter. Sergeant. Drowned in the sinking of the Pere de Famille February 17, 1770, returning to France.

MORIN, PIERRE
Died Noember 8, 1751.

MORION, JEAN
Royal carpenter. Died August 8, 1738.

MORTALLE, JEAN CLAUDE
Discharged September 15, 1763, roll of January 1, 1763, folio 17.

MOTTA, ANASTASE

MOUCHETTE, EUGENE
Died.

MOUILLARD, FRANCOIS
With half-pay of 6 livres per month according to a decision of April 4, 1764, sent to the Bureau des Invalides April 5, 1764. Discharged September 15, 1763.

MOULARD, JEAN
Company of Vaugine. Discharged February 6, 1770, with half-pay of 4 livres 10 sols per month according to a decision of July 16, 1771, payable in Paris.

MOULINS, LOUIS

MOUSSEAU, FRANCOIS
Died at the hospital January 11, 1759. See the roll of June 1, 1760, folio 4.

MOUTON, PHILIPPES
Discharged September 15, 1763, roll of January 1, 1763, folio 19.

MOUZA or MOUSSA, PIERRE
Discharged September 15, 1763, roll of January 1, 1763, folio 10.

MOZAQUE, ETIENNE
Discharged June 1, 1756.

MURAT, GAEZARD
Deserted June 15, 1756.

MURAT, CLAUDE
Deserted July 17, 1755.

LOUISIANA TROOPS —:— 1720-1770

NABOT, JEAN

NADAL, JEAN

NANOTTE, CHARLES VINCENT
Died at the hospital January 24, 1758. See the roll of July 1, 1760, folio 8.

NANTAIS, FRANCOIS

NARBONNE, ANTOINE
Discharged September 15, 1763, roll of Januarry 1, 1763, folio 17.

NARCIS, DENIS
Died October 24, 1751.

NAUD, EMERY
Deserted June 30, 1750.

NAUVACOU or NOWACK, JEAN BAPTISTE
Discharged October 8, 1769, roll of January 1, 1763, folio 43.

NAVARON, FRANCOIS
Corporal. Drowned in the sinking of the Pere de Famille February 17, 1770, returning to France.

NAVET, JULLIEN

NAVET, JULIEN
Corporal. Drowned in the sinking of the Pere de Famille February 17, 1770, returning to France.

NEMINGRE, ANDRÉ

NEMINGRE or NEMINGER, ANTOINE
Discharged September 15, 1763, roll of January 1, 1763, folio 17.

NESICK, MATHIEU
Died at Illinois November 20, 1754, company of Neyon.

NEVEU, CLAUDE
Drowned in the sinking of the Pere de Famille February 17, 1770, returning to France.

NEVEU, FRANCOIS
Discharged February 6, 1770, company of Duplessis.

NEVEU, JULLIEN
Died at New Orleans September 4, 1757, company of Chabert.

NEVEUX, FRANCOIS

NEYON
Cadet soldat. Died in October 1755, company of Neyon.

NEYRAND, ANTOINE
Discharged September 15, 1763, roll of January 1, 1763, folio 5.

NEZAIR, CHARLES
Condemned to the gallies June 3, 1750.

NIBOUILLET, ANTOINE
Deserted April 15, 1755.

NICAISE, JEAN BAPTISTE
Discharged May 1, 1750.

NICOLAS, HUGUES

NICOLAS, JEAN

NICOLAS, JOSEPH

NICOLEAU, LOUIS
Drowned in the sinking of the Pere de Famille February 17, 1770, returning to France.

NICOLET, JEAN
Called La Roze. Corporal in the company of Reggio. Killed in the burning of Arkansas Fort by Jean Baptiste Bernard, soldier, of the same company, who obtained pardon from Monsieur de Kerlerec by his letter of September 12, 1756.

NICOLLE, JEAN
Killed by Indians April 20, 1750.

NICOLLE, LOUIS
Died February 8, 1751.

NICOLLET, JOSEPH
Died at New Orleans February 9, 1766, roll of January 1, 1763, folio 34.

NIOLET, PIERRE
Discharged November 16, 1769, roll of January 1, 1769, folio 40.

NIOLON, JEAN
Hanged June 4, 1756, company of Mazan.

NIVOIX, HONORÉ SEBASTIEN
(Died October 14, 1751?)

NOIR, MICHEL JOSEPH
Drowned in the sinking of the Pere de Famille February 17, 1770, returning to France.

NOIRET, JOSEPH
Died October 14, 1751.

LOUISIANA TROOPS —:— 1720-1770

NOIZET, HUBERT
Discharged October 17, 1751.

NOLLET, FRANCOIS
Discharged September 30, 1769, roll of January 1, 1769 folio 50.

NOMBRE, JEAN ANTOINE
Discharged September 15, 1763, with half-pay of 6 livres per month according to a decision of April 4, 1764, sent to the Bureau des Invalides April 5, 1764.

NORMAND, ANTOINE
With half-pay of 6 livres per month according to a decision of April 4, 1764, sent to the Bureau des Invalides April 5, 1764.

NORMAND, PIERRE
Deserted January 1, 1757.

NORRITTE, FRANCOIS
Died at the hospital December 15, 1754, company of Villiers.

NOUILLER, JOSEPH
Strangled himself in prison March 15, 1756, company of La Tour.

NOURRY, ANDRÉ
Died at Illinois January 15, 1765, roll of January 1, 1763, folio 31.

NOUSPAON, LOUIS
Drummer. With half-pay of 6 livres per month according to a decision of April 4, 1764, sent to the Bureau des Invalides April 5, 1764.

NOUVEAU, LOUIS
Discharged October 31, 1769, roll of January 1, 1763, folio 46.

NOYEL, FRANCOIS
Died April 15, 1754, company of Des Varennes.

NUGNOT, JULIEN

NYERRE, PIERRE FRANCOIS
Sergeant. Discharged March 4, 1769, with half-pay of 10 livres per month, payable at Valenciennes, according to a decision of September 3, 1769, sent to the Bureau des Invalides. He is from Bouchain.

LOUISIANA TROOPS —:— 1720-1770

OBERVILLE, PIERRE

OCK, MICHEL
Went to France on the Samson October 1, 1769, roll of January 1, 1763, folio 48.

OLDRIN, PIERRE

OLLIVIER, JEAN
Discharged September 15, 1763, roll of January 1, 1763, folio 24.

OLLIVIER, JOSEPH

OLLIVIER, NICOLAS
Died at the hospital November 20, 1766, roll of January 1, 1763, folio 33.

ONTRA, JOSEPH
Died August 16, 1736. The death certificate is at the Bureau.

ORÉ, JEAN

ORNSTEINN, SERVAIS
Discharged October 31, 1769, roll of January 1, 1763, folio 45.

OUALLE, ANTOINE

OUARDIER, LOUIS
Died at Akancas March 25, 1757, company of Reggio.

OUDABLE, ALEXANDRE
Discharged June 1, 1751.

OUDEL, THIERRY
Deserted, company of Terrepuy.

OUFROY, CHARLES GUILLEAUME
Drowned in Bayou St. Jean January 31, 1769, roll of January 1, 1763, folio 38.

OURIEZ, LOUIS
Discharged June 1, 1751.

OVEL, JEAN BAPTISTE
Discharged June 1, 1764, roll of January 1, 1763, folio 28.

LOUISIANA TROOPS —:— 1720-1770

PABOEUF, FRANCOIS
PADET, JEAN
PAGE, GUILLEAUME
Discarged September 15, 1763, roll of January 1, 1763, folio 2.
PAILLET, GUILLEAUME
Discharged September 15, 1763, roll of January 1, 1763, folio 22.
PAILLET, JEAN
discharged September 30, 1769, roll of January 1, 1763, folio 55. Canoneer engaged in 1767.
PAIN, HUGUES
Deserted October 21, 1761.
PAINDAVOINE, NICOLAS JOSEPH JEROME
Died December 31, 1765, roll of January 1, 1763, folio 31.
PAJET, FRANCOIS
Died July 25, 1735.
PAJET, FRANCOIS
Discharged October 6, 1769, roll of January 1, 1763, folio 38.
PAJOT or PAJET, JEAN
Died December 6, 1738.
PAJOT or PAGOT, LOUIS
Died at the hospital November 13, 1766, roll of January 1, 1763, folio 83.
PAJOT, MARIN
Died August 13, 1745, company of Membrede.
PALIS, FRANCOIS
Died August 4, 1738.
PAMEL, FRANCOIS
PANET, MATHIEU
PANNIER, LOUIS
With half-pay of 4 livres 10 sols per month according to a decision of April 4, 1764, sent to the Bureau des Invalides April 5, 1764.
PANQUINET, LOUIS
PAPION, JAC
Died April 10, 1738.
PAPILLON, JACQUES
PAQUIER, JEAN
Discharged June 24, 1751.
PAQUIN, JEAN
Deserted June 30, 1750.

PARADIS, MARIN
Discharged September 15, 1763, roll of January 1, 1763, folio 1.
PARAUD, BENOIST
PARAUD, BENOIST
Drowned in the sinking of the Pere de Famille February 17, 1770, returning to France.
PARAUD, NICOLAS
Deserted June 8, 1756.
PARISY, CLAUDE
Died at Mobile September 8, 1754, company of Villemont.
PARISY, PIERRE
Died at the hospital April 19, 1757. See the roll of June 1, 1760, folio 2.
PARISY, PIERRE
Died at New Orleans April 19, 1757, company of de la Houssaye.
PARLAT, JEAN
Discharged September 15, 1763, roll of January 1, 1763, folio 2.
PARMENTIER, DOMINIQUE
Executed by the firing squad at Mobile September 6, 1757, company of Paupulus.
PARON, GABRIEL
PARPILLAUD, CHARLES
Deserted April 27, 1761. See the roll of the same year, folio 12.
PASCAL, LEONARD
PASQUIER, CHARLES THEODORE
PASQUIER, JEAN FRANCOIS
PASQUIER, JEAN FRANCOIS
Died at La Balize September 30, 1767, roll of January 1, 1763, folio 35.
PASTOR, FRANCOIS

LOUISIANA TROOPS —:— 1720-1770

PASTOR, FRANCOIS
Discharged February 6, 1770, with half-pay of 12 livres per month according to a decision of April 28, 1770. Died March 1, 1770, at the hospital of La Rochelle. The death certificate is attached to a letter of Monsieur Le Moyne and was placed in the rolls of the Isle of Re for the month of July, 1770.

PATRICE, JACQUES
Discharged April 18, 1756, went to France on the Messager.

PAUJERET, PIERRE

PAUL, CHARLES
Discharged November 30, 1751.

PAUL, JEAN

PAULET, ANTOINE
Discharged May 1, 1750.

PAURÉ or POIRAY, EUGENE
Licensed at Le Havre. See the general roll of February 22, 1761, sent from that port. Received half-pay carried to 12 livres per month according to a decision of January 29, 1762, sent the same day to the Bureau des Invalides. This sergeant is named Eugene Joseph Pouree, according to his baptism certificate that he presented.

PAUSSÉ, JEAN
Discharged September 15, 1763, roll of January 1, 1763, folio 8.

PAYER, JEAN
Died at the hospital February 19, 1757, company of Bellenos.

PEJA, JEAN
Died in 1738, in (the company of) Benoist.

PEIGNIER, FRANCOIS
Died at the hospital March 6, 1767, roll of January 1, 1763, folio 34.

PEILLE, ANTOINE
Sergeant. With half-pay of 20 livres per month, according to a decision of April 4, 1764, sent to the Bureau des Invalides April 5, 1764.

PELIGAUD, ANDRÉ

PELISSIER, ETIENNE
Died at the hospital May 24, 1754, company of Arazola.

PELLERIN, CHARLES
Condemned by contumacy for desertion. See the record of September 30, 1753.

PELLERIN, GIRARD
Died April 9, 1737.

PELTIER, ANDRÉ
Discharged September 15, 1763, roll of January 1, 1763, folio 6.

PELTIER, NICOLAS
Discharged April 18, 1756, went to France.

PELUSSET, JOSEPH
Died December 7, 1754, company of Macarty.

PENNE, JEAN
Died at Mobile December 18, 1754, company of Grandechamp.

PENTINETTE, LOUIS
Discharged Septemebr 1, 1750.

PEOCQUEMANE, CANTELIP (?)

PEPIN, JEAN
Discharged March 1, 1764, roll of January 1, 1763, folio 29.

PERAULT, JEAN FRANCOIS
Died at Mobile October 9, 1755, company of La Gautraye.

PERCHEL, PIERRE

PERCHETTE, PIERRE
Discharged May 24, 1756.

PERDIGAUX, JEAN

PERDIGAUX, JEAN
Died at the hospital May 14, 1754, company of Chavois.

PERDIGNAN, JACQUES
Fifer, company of Benoist, died November 12, 1764, roll of January 1, 1763, folio 26.

PERELLE, MATHURIN

PERET, PIERRE
Discharged February 6, 1770, with half-pay of 4 livres 10 sols per month according to a decision of April 28, 1770.

PERETTE, CLAUDE
Died September 3, 1751.

PERICHAUD, LEONARD
Habitant since August 5, 1753.

LOUISIANA TROOPS —:— 1720-1770

PERICHE, PHILIPPES
Discharged September 15, 1763, roll of January 1, 1763, folio 14.
PERIEO, GUILLEAUME
Deserted March 1, 1763, roll of January 1, 1763, folio 22.
PERIGOIS, MICHEL
Died October 10, 1751.
PERIOUX, JACQUES
Habitant since June 1, 1754.
PERNAY, JEAN
Drowned in the river August 26, 1756, company of Neyon.
PERNOUS, CLAUDE
Discharged August 18, 1751.
PEROLET, ANTOINE
PERON, FRANCOIS
Company of Villiers, discharged February 6, 1770.
PEROT, ETIENNE JOSEPH
Died at the hospital April 1, 1767, roll of January 1, 1763, folio 35.
PERRAUT, JOSEPH
PERRET, PIERRE
PERRETTE OR PARRET, JEAN CLAUDE
Died March 22, 1768, roll of January 1, 1763, folio 36.
PERRETTE, PIERRE
Discharged September 15, 1763, roll of January 1, 1763, folio 23.
PERRIER, PAUL
PERRIERS, PIERRE
Drowned at Natchez November 19, 1754, company of Grandchamp.
PERRIN, CLAUDE
Discharged. See the roll dated at Calais May 2, 1763.
PERRIN, DAVID JEAN
Died November 19, 1751.
PERRON, LOUIS
PERSIGNAC, FRANCOIS
Drowned in the river while descending from Natchez October 2, 1754, company of Murat.
PESCHE, PIERRE
Discharged June 30, 1751.

PESCHE, URBAIN
Extended leave November 11, 1758. See the roll of June 1, 1760, folio 2.
PETAUT, GUILLEAUME
Died at the hospital September 15, 1755, company of Chavois.
PETITLOUCHE, BERTRAND
Discharged August 16, 1756.
PETIT, EUGENE
Corporal. Drowned in the sinking of the Pere de Famille February 17, 1770, returning to France.
PETIT, FOELIX
Died at Pointe Coupee November 5, 1754, company of Grandpre.
PETIT, JUDE
Discharged February 6, 1770, company of Duplessis.
PETITDIDIER, CLAUDE
Corporal. Discharged September 15, 1763, roll of Jaunary 1, 1763, folio 4, decision of April 4, 1764, for half-pay of 4 livres per month, sent to the Bureau des Invalides April 5, 1764.
PETITJEAN, MARTIN
With half-pay of 6 livres per month according to a decision of April 4, 1764, sent to the Bureau des Invalides April 5, 1764.
PEUJAT, FRANCOIS
Discharged June 1, 1764, roll of January 1, 1763, folio 27.
PHARAMOND, PIERRE
Died at Natchez September 30, 1754, company of Montberault.
PHILIBERT, ETIENNE
PIAN, MATHIEU
Discharged August 10, 1754.

LOUISIANA TROOPS —:— 1720-1770

PIAU, ABEL
Died at the Isle of Re January 30, 1770. See the roll of Monsieur Giraud of the Isle of Re for the month of January, 1770. The death certificate is attached to a letter of Monsieur Le Moyne and was placed in the files of the Isle of Re for the month of July, 1770. Company of de Vaugine.

PICARD, JACQUES
Died December 15, 1745, company of de Blanc.

PICARD, JEAN
Corporal. Drowned in the sinking of the Pere de Famille February 17, 1770, returning to France.

PICARD, JEAN FRANCOIS

PICARD, LOUIS
Licensed at Le Havre. See the general roll of February 22, 1761, sent from that port. He received half-pay.

PICHON, JULIEN
Died December 21, 1737.

PICON, JOSEPH
Died at Akancas April 11, 1756, company of Murat.

PICOTTIN, CHARLES
Died October 28, 1751.

PIDOLEAU, PIERRE
Discarged September 15, 1763, roll of January 1, 1763, folio 24.

PIEN, MATHURIN

PIER, JEAN
Died October 20, 1751.

PIERRIL, LAZARRE
Discharged June 1, 1751.

PIGNANA, DIEGO
Deserted April 26, 1755.

PIGNON, CLAUDE

PILLEVERT, JULLIEN
Deserted in 1754.

PILLIARD, CLAUDE

PILLIAU or PILLIOT, ABEL
Went to France on the Samson October 18, 1769, roll of January 1, 1763, folio 47.

PILLIAU, LEOPOL
Died at the hospital October 22, 1769, roll of January 1, 1763, folio 50.

PILLIÉ, PIERRE
Extended leave and went to France on the royal vessel La Fortune January 1, 1759. See the roll of June 1, 1760, folio 7.

PINCEMAIL, LOUIS NOEL PAUL
Discharged September 1, 1764, roll of January 1, 1764, folio 26. Re-engaged in 1767, discharged October 8, 1769.

PINEAU, JEAN
Died October 6, 1756, company of Artaud.

PINGET, PIERRE
Executed by the firing squad September 6, 1751.

PINTER, JOSEPH
Deserted September 28, 1769, roll of January 1, 1763, folio 52.

PIOCHET, JEAN BAPTISTE

PIOT, FRANCOIS
Deserted September, 1769, roll of January 1, 1763, folio 37.

PIRION, MATHIEU
Executed by the firing squad July 31, 1750.

PITEL, JACQUES ETIENNE
Drowned while descending from Natchez October 2, 1754, company of Hazeur.

PIVOTEAU, GUILLEAUME
With half-pay of 4 livres 10 sols per month according to a decision of June 11, 1764, sent to the Bureau des Invalides June 12, 1764. Discharged September 15, 1763, roll of January 1, 1763, folio 5.

PLACET, ANTOINE
Discharged December 1 1767, roll of January 1, 1763, folio 35.

PLAUTIN, THOMAS
Died at the hospital June 4, 1764, roll of January 1, 1763, folio 29.

LOUISIANA TROOPS —:— 1720-1770

PLESMIN, JEAN
Discharged August 18, 1751.

PLOTTIER, LOUIS
Died September 23, 1750.

PLOYARD, NICOLAS
Drowned at Ouabache November 10, 1756, company of La Gautraye.

PLUMET, FRANCOIS
Discharged August 1, 1765, roll of January 1, 1763, folio 30.

POIRÉ, ANTOINE
Discarged December 31, 1764, roll of January 1, 1763, folio 26.

POIRÉ, EDMÉ LUCIEN
Died while on leave in France.

POIRIER, JEAN ETIENNE
Died at Mobile December 9, 1759. See the roll of June 1, 1760, company of Bonnille.

POIRSON, JEAN BAPTISTE

POISSON, JACQUES
Drowned July 27, 1764, roll of January 1, 1763, folio 27.

POITEVIN, RENÉ
With half-pay of 6 livres per month according to a decision of April 4, 1764 sent to the Bureau des Invalides April 5, 1764. Discharged September 15, 1763.

POITIER, RENÉ
Died at the hospital June 1, 1754, company of Derneville.

POLIAN, JACQUES

POLIAN, CAEZAR
Deserted October 15, 1761. See the roll of the same year, folio 46.

POLMANNE, GEORGES
Discharged September 15, 1763. Sergeant with half-pay of 15 livres per month according to a decision of April 4, 1764, sent to the Bureau des Invalides April 5, 1764.

POMMARD, JACQUES

POMMARD, JACQUES
Discarged July 16, 1756.

PONGE, JEAN
Discharged September 15, 1763, roll of January 1, 1763, folio 14.

PONTIF or PONTIS, FRANCOIS
Abandonné aux Troupes de Cerre. Lettre de Mgr. a Mr. Hocquart a Brest du'Bre 1760.

PONTMAIRE or POULMAIRE JEAN
With half-pay of 4 livres 10 sols per month according to a decision of April 4, 1764, sent to the Bureau des Invalides April 5, 1764.

PORET, JEAN
Discharged September 15, 1763, roll of January 1, 1763, folio 14.

PORSON, JEAN BAPTISTE
Died February 18, 1751.

PORTAY, FRANCOIS
Discharged September 15, 1763, roll of January 1, 1763, folio 16.

PORTIER, MATHIEU

PORTIERS, PIERRE

PORTRON, ANDRÉ
Died at the hospital October 27, 1759. See the roll of June 1, 1760, folio 5.

PORTIER, PIERRE
Drowned in the sinking of the Pere de Famille February 17, 1770, returning to France.

POTTIER, MATHURIN
Sergeant. Discharged February 6, 1770, with half-pay of 9 livres per month, according to a decision of April 28, 1770.

POTTIN, FRANCOIS

POUILLARD, JACQUES JOSEPH
Discharged September 15, 1763, roll of January 1, 1763, folio 26.

POULIN, JEAN
Died March 29, 1751.

POULIN, PIERRE
Discharged July 22, 1751.

POULMAN, JEAN
Discharged September 15, 1763, roll of January 1, 1763, folio 6.

LOUISIANA TROOPS —:— 1720-1770

POULIQUIN or POLICAIN,
JACQUES
Discharged September 15, 17-63, roll of January 1, 1763, folio 7.

POUSIN, JEAN LAMBERT
Went to France on the Samson October 1, 1769, roll of January 1, 1763, folio 52.

POUSSAIN, JEAN LAMBERT
Sergeant. Discharged February 6, 1770, with half-pay of 12 livres per month according to a decision of April 28, 1770.

POUSSEL, ETIENNE
Died July 20, 1737.

POUSSINGRE, LEOPOL

PRADES, JEAN
Discharged September 30, 17-59, roll of January 1, 1763, folio 54.

PRADIER, JOSEPH

PREVOST, ANTOINE

PREVOST, CLAUDE ANTOINE

PREVOST, CLAUDE ANTOINE
Died at Arkancas May 23, 17-59. See the roll of June 1, 1760, folio 10.

PREVOST, JEAN
Died October 4, 1750.

PREVOST, MICHEL
Died at Akancas July 20, 17-54, company of La Tour.

PREVOST, SIMON
Drowned while ascending to Pointe Coupee March 4, 1754, company of Villemont.

PRIÉ, ANTOINE

PRIOUX, MICHEL

PRISSER or PRIESLER, JOSEPH
Discharged September 15, 17-63, roll of January 1, 1763, folio 18.

PRIVÉE, DENIS
Killed or taken by the Cherakis or Chikachas at Fort Ouabache November 9, 1757, company of Trant.

PROGIN, JACQUES
Died October 8, 1751.

PROU, FRANCOIS

PROU, JEAN
Died at the hospital August 14, 1758. See the roll of June 1, 1760, folio 7.

PROUT, LOUIS BARTHELEMY
Discharged October 1, 1768, roll of January 1, 1763, folio 33.

PROUX, NICOLAS
Corporal. Died September 4, 1758, of wounds received the same day. See the criminal proceedings against Pierre Flamant in the files of Louisiana.

PRUDHOMME, ANTOINE
GAUDIER
See the "G" section.

PRUDHOMME, ANTOINE
GAUDIER

PRUDHOMME, JACQUES

PRUDHOMME, JEAN
Discharged September 15, 17-63, roll of January 1, 1768, folio 18.

PRUDHOMME, PIERRE
Discharged April 1, 1750.

PRUDHOMME, PIERRE
SEBASTIEN
Discharged September 15, 17-63, roll of January 1, 1763, folio 8.

PUELLE, VICTOR
Discharged June 30, 1768, roll of January 1, 1763, folio 36.

PUIGRAND, ANTOINE
Went to Santo Domingo on the vessel Aigrette July 22, 1763, roll of January 1, 1763, folio 3.

PUSSEAU, PIERRE

QUARTIER, JEAN PIERRE
With half-pay of 6 livres per month according to a decision of April 4, 1764, sent to the Bureau des Invalides April 5, 1764.

QUELLIER, FRANCOIS
Died April 20, 1751.

QUENET, PIERRE

QUENTEL, PIERRE
Corporal. With half-pay of 12 livres per month according to a decision of April 4, 1764, sent to the Bureau des Invalides.

QUESTRE, GEORGES
Discarged April 1, 1765, roll of January 1, 1763, folio 82.

LOUISIANA TROOPS —:— 1720-1770

RABIGO, JEAN LOUIS
 Discharged September 15, 1763, roll of January 1, 1763, folio 21.
RABY, PIERRE
 Discharged April 1, 1756.
RACHAL, BARTHELEMY
 Discharged September 15, 1763, roll of January 1, 1763, folio 12.
RACHAL, JEAN
RACHAL, LOUIS
 Discharged September 15, 1763, roll of January 1, 1763, folio 24.
RACHAL, PIERRE
 Died at Natchez April 19, 1756, company of Des Mazelliers.
RACLOT, CLAUDE
 Sergeant. With half-pay of 15 livres per month according to a decision of April 4, 1764, sent to the Bureau des Invalides April 5, 1764. Discharged September 15, 1763, roll of January 1, 1763, folio 4.
RAFFINE, JEAN
 Deserted November 20, 1761. See the roll of the same year, folio 5.
RAGON, GUILLEAUME
RAINGOT, SIMON
 Died at the hospital October 24, 1769, roll of January 1, 1763, folio 38.
RAISON, JEAN
RAISON, JEAN
 Discharged February 6, 1770, company of Mazelliere.
RAMBAUD, PIERRE
 Discharged September 15, 1763, roll of January 1, 1763, folio 5.
RAMBIN, ANDRÉ
RAMELOT, LAMBERT
 Discharged September 15, 1763, roll of January 1, 1763, folio 21.
RANGÉ, JACQUES
 Drowned while descending from Natchez October 20, 1754, company of Gaumont.

RAOUL, JEAN
 Discharged May 1, 1751.
RASSERET, JEAN
 Died at Mobile February 26, 1756, company of Bonnille.
RAUX, PIERRE
RAUX, PIERRE
 Discharged February 6, 1770, with half-pay of 4 livres 10 sols per month according to a decision of April 28, 1770. Died at the hospital of the Isle of Re April 29, 1770. The death certificate is attached to a letter of Monsieur Le Moyne and placed in the records of Monsieur de Repentigny, Isle of Re for the month of July, 1770.
RAVERDY, MARC
 Died October 24, 1751.
RAYMOND, PIERRE
 Discharged September 15, 1763, roll of January 1, 1763, folio 16.
REAUX or RAUX, PIERRE
 Discharged September 15, 1763, roll of January 1, 1763, folio 20.
REBLINQUE, JEAN
 Killed August 14, 1746, company of Terreplvy.
REDON, GUILLEAUME
 Condemned by contumacy for desertion. See the proceedings of September 30, 1753.
REDON, PIERRE
 Extended leave. Went to France on the royal vessel La Fortune January 1, 1759. See the roll of June 1, 1760, folio 12.
REGNARD, JEAN BAPTISTE
REGNIER, CHARLES
REGNIER, LOUIS
 Drowned in the river, June 20, 1755, company of Aubry.
REMEGAUD, SIMON
REMY, FRANCOIS
 Died at the hospital November 22, 1757, company of Chabert.
REMY, JEAN
RENAL, JEAN

RENAL, JEAN
Discharged February 6, 1770, with half-pay of 6 livres per month, according to a decision of April 28, 1770.

RENANDS, JEAN BAPTISTE

RENARD, FRANCOIS

RENARDY, JOSEPH

RENAULT, CLAUDE JOSEPH
Died June 3, 1738.

RENAUD, JACQUES
Drowned while descending from Natchez October 2, 1754, company of Macarty.

RENAUD, JEAN BAPTISTE
Discharged September 15, 1763, roll of January 1, 1763, folio 19.

RENAUD, JEAN JOSEPH
Died at the hospital October 27, 1756, company of Arazola.

RENAUD, JEAN LOUIS DENIS
Deserted April 26, 1755

RENAUD, PIERRE
Discharged September 15, 1763, roll of January 1, 1763, folio 9.

RENAUDA, ANTOINE
Died July 21, 1756, company of Aubry.

RENNEPONT, ETIENNE

RENOIRE, JEAN LOUIS

RÉPAIRE, NICOLAS FRANCOIS
Discharged February 1, 1764, roll of January 1, 1763, folio 29.

REPMENTER, ABRAHAM
Discharged October 8, 1769, roll of January 1, 1763, folio 35.

REQUIEM, CHARLES
Died March 12, 1750.

RESTE, PIERRE LOUIS

RETZ, PIERRE LOUIS
Discharged September 15, 1763, roll of January 1, 1763, folio 23.

REYNE, JEAN BAPTISTE

RICHARD, GEORGES

RICHARD, JACQUES
Died November 27, 1750

RICHARD, JEAN
Discharged September 15, 1763, roll of January 1, 1763, folio 8

RICHARD, PIERRE
Drowned in the river July 27, 1754, company of Favrot.

RICHAUD, GEORGES

RICHAUME, GEORGES
Discharged February 6, 1770, with half-pay of 4 livres per month according to a decision of April 21, 1770.

RICHÉ, MAURICE
Killed or taken at the Ouabache Fort by the Cherakis or Chicachas, November 19, 1757, company of Aubry.

RICORTIER, JEAN
Condemned by contumacy to be broken on the wheel, according to a decision of the council of war for having killed his (commanding) officer June 7, 1757, company of Gourdon.

RIGOLET, JOSEPH
Died October 16, 1735.

RINGAUD, MARC
Discharged February 6, 1770, with half-pay of 4 livres 10 sols per month according to a decision of April 28, 1770.

RIOL, FRANCOIS
Died May 15, 1745, company of Chavois.

RIOT, JEAN

RIQUET, PIERRE
With half-pay of 9 livres per month according to a decision of December 12, 1764, sent to the Bureau des Invalides the same day. Corporal, company of Trudeau. Discharged July 1, 1764.

RIQUOY, SIMON

RISSÉ, JEAN
Discharged September 15, 1763, roll of January 1, 1763, folio 24.

RIVARDE, JEAN BAPTISTE

RIVOIS, JEAN
Discharged November 31, 1769, remained at Arcankas, roll of January 1, 1763, folio 48.

LOUISIANA TROOPS —:— 1720-1770

ROBAILLE, JEAN
Discarged July 16, 1756, went to France.

ROBERT, FRANCOIS

ROBERT, FRANCOIS
Discarged February 6, 1770, with half-pay of 4 livres 10 sols per month, according to a decision of April 28, 1770.

ROBERT, GABRIEL
Died December 31, 1754, company of Chabert.

ROBERT, JEAN

ROBIER, JEAN
Discharged October 31, 1769, roll of January 1, 1763, floio 51.

ROBINE, JULIEN
Discharged April 18, 1756, went to France.

ROBINET, FRANCOIS
With half-pay of 9 livres per month according to a decision of September 22, 1763, sent to the Bureau des Invalides September 22, 1763.

ROBINET, JEAN LOUIS

ROBINOT, RENÉ
Died December 23, 1754, company of De Varennes.

ROCABOIS, ANTOINE
Died December 26, 1751.

ROCHE, CLAUDE

ROCHE, JEAN JACQUES
Went to France October 1, 1763, roll of January 1, 1763, folio 26.

ROCHEFORT, PIERRE
Died at the hospital October 26, 1765, roll of January 1, 1763, folio 30.

ROCHER, JEAN
Discharged September 15, 1763, roll of January 1, 1763, folio 8.

ROCHET, PHILIPPES
Discharged July 10, 1755, and returned to France on the Rhinoceros.

ROCHETEAU, RENÉ AYMÉ
Discharged July 23, 1751.

RODES, JACQUES
Discharged September 15, 1763, roll of January 1, 1763, folio 14.

ROGER, JEAN

ROHAN, ANTOINE
Executed by the firing squad for desertion January 27, 1741, following a process-verbal attached to a letter of Monsieur Scimars de Belleisle, April 28, 1741.

ROLAND, JEAN

ROLAND or ROOLIN, MICHEL
Discharged May 1, 1751.

ROLEIN, JEAN CLAUDE
Deserted September 1, 1754.

ROLLET, HENRY
Discharged September 15, 1763, roll of January 1, 1763, folio 14.

ROLET, MICHEL

ROLIN, PIERRE
Drowned at La Balize January 10, 1754, company of La Tour.

ROLLAND, CHARLES GUILLEAUME
Died December 6, 1745, company of Membrede.

ROMAIN, LAMBERT
Discharged June 1, 1751.

ROMBDIERE, FRANCOIS
Discharged June 1, 1751.

RONDEAU, RENÉ

RONDEAU, RENÉ
Discharged February 6, 1770, company of Mazelliere.

RONDEAU, RENÉ
Went o France on the vessel Samson October 1, 1769, roll of January 1, 1763, folio 38.

RONDELON, FRANCOIS
Died September 30, 1738.

RONDET, PIERRE JOSEPH
Died at the hospital November 12, 1757, company of Benoist.

ROSE, ROE SOU JACQUES
Discharged September 15, 1763, roll of January 1, 1763, folio 12.

ROSTY, ANTOINE
Died, company of Terrepuy. The date of his death is not on the roll sent.

LOUISIANA TROOPS —:— 1720-1770

ROSSY or ROUSSY JEAN BAPTISTE
Sergeant with half-pay of 16 livres per month according to a decision of June 26, 1765. sent to the Bureau des Invalides June 27, 1765. Discharged September 15, 1763.

ROUBEAU, JOSEPH

ROUBELAIS, JEAN
Discharged September 15, 1763, roll of January 1, 1763, folio 18.

ROUENCE, CLAUDE

ROUGET, ETIENNE

ROUJEOT, LOUIS
Died at the hospital August 15, 1755, company of Bonnille.

ROULLAND, PIERRE JOSEPH
Discharged November 30, 1769, roll of January 1, 1763, folio 51.

ROURIERE, JEAN
Discharged September 15, 1763, roll of January 1, 1763, folio 19.

ROUSSEAU, PIERRE
Died August 14, 1746, company of Gauvrit.

ROUSSEL, CLAUDE
Discharged October 8, 1769, roll of January 1, 1763, folio 49.

ROUSSEL, DENIS
With half-pay of 4 livres 10 sols per month according to a decision of April 4, 1764, sent to the ureau des Invalides April 5, 1764.

ROUSSEL, FRANCOIS

ROUSSEL, JEAN

ROUSSEL, JEAN
With half-pay of 12 livres per month according to a decision of April 4, 1764, sent to the Bureau des Invalides April 5, 1764. Discharged November 15, 1763, roll of January 1, 1763, filio 2. Sergeant.

ROUSSEL, JEAN
Discharged September 15, 1763, roll of January 1, 1763, folio 5.

ROUSSEL, PAUL

ROUSSELOT, ANTOINE

ROUSSEVE, JEAN BAPTISTE MAURICE

ROUX, JACQUES
Died September 18, 1751.

ROUYEUSE, CLAUDE

ROY, CLAUDE JOSEPH
Died at the hospital June 8, 1754, company of Sommes.

ROY, JEAN
Died August 19, 1736.

ROY, PIERRE
With half-pay of 9 livres per month according to a decision rendered at Compiegne July 19, 1764, sent to the Bureau des Invalides July 24, 1764.

ROYAUX, ALEXANDRE
Discharged October 8, 1769, roll of January 1 ,1763, folio 47.

ROYER, CLAUDE
Deserted July 19, 1755.

ROYER, JEAN
Discharged September 15, 1763, roll of January 1, 1763, folio 7.

ROYER, JEAN
Died September 23, 1751.

ROYER, JEAN BAPTISTE
Deserted November 3, 1754, company of Derneville.

ROYER, NICOLAS
Discharged September 15, 1763, roll of January 1, 1763, folio 8.

ROYER, PIERRE

ROYER, PIERRE
With half-pay of 6 livres per month according to a decision of April 4, 1764, sent to the Bureau des Invalides April 5, 1764. Discharged September 15, 1763.

ROZE, JACQUES
With half-pay of 6 livres per month according to a decision of April 4, 1764, sent to the Bureau des Invalides April 5, 1764.

ROZIER, LEONARD

LOUISIANA TROOPS —:— 1720-1770

ROZIER, LEONARD

Corporal. Discharged February 6, 1770, with half-pay of 6 livres per month, according to a decision of April 28, 1770.

RUFFIER, FRANCOIS

With half-pay of 15 livres per month according to a decision of April 4, 1764, sent to the Bureau des Invalides April 5, 1764. Sergeant, discharged September 15, 1763.

SABATIER, JOSEPH
Discharged May 1, 1751.

SABATTIER, JEAN
Drowned in the sinking of the Pere de Famille February 17, 1770, returning to France.

SABOTTE or SOBOT, GUILLEAUME ETIENNE
Discharged September 15, 1763, roll of January 1, 1763, folio 10.

ST. AGNÈS, PIERRE

ST. AIGNE, PIERRE
Deserted August 30, 1761. See the roll of the same year, folio 40.

ST. DIZIER, ETIENNE

ST. GERMAIN, PIERRE
Died January 27, 1739.

ST. JACQUES
With half-pay of 9 livres per month according to a decision of June 11, 1764, sent to the Bureau des Invalides June 12, 1764.

ST. JULLIEN, LOUIS
With half-pay of 6 livres per month according to a decision of April 8, 1764, sent to the Bureau des Invalides April 5, 1764.

ST. PIERRE
Died March 19, 1744, company of Le Verrier.

SALINS or SALEM, MATHIEU
Discharged September 15, 1763, roll of January 1, 1763, folio 22.

SALVIN, JEAN

SALVAN, JEAN
Discharged September 30, 1769, roll of January 1, 1763, folio 37.

SAMBLOT or SAUBOLT, BENOIST
Discharged September 30, 1764, folio 51, roll of January 1, 1763.

SAMUEL, JEAN BAPTISTE
Discharged October 1, 1764, roll of January 1, 1763, folio 29.

SANTÉ, JEAN
Died at New Orleans March 26, to the Bureau des Invalides A-folio 31.

SANTRÉ, FRANCOIS

SANVILLE, CLAUDE

SARAMAIQUE, RENAUD
Discharged September 15, 1763, roll of January 1, 1763, folio 1.

SARLAT, JEAN

SARRAZIN, FRANCOIS

SAUCIER, FRANCOIS

SAULET, LOUIS FRANCOIS

SAUNIER, FRANCOIS
Died September 2, 1731.

SAUNIER, PIERRE

SAUSSARD, PIERRE CLAUDE MALO
Died September 7, 1751

SAUSSÉ, JEAN
With half-pay of 9 livres per month according to a decision of April 9, 1772

SAUTIER or SAINTIER FRANCOIS
Discharged September 15, 1763, roll of January 1, 1763, folio 25

SAUTRAIS, FRANCOIS
Discharged September 15, 1763, roll of January 1, 1763, folio 21

SAUTRAU, CLAUDE
Deserted June 8, 1755

SAUVILLE, CLAUDE
Discharged August 20, 1770, with half-pay of 9 livres per month according to a decision of October 17, 1770. Drummer.

SAVANT, MATHIEU
Discharged March 19, 1755.

SAVER, JEAN PHILIPPES
Died October 1, 1751.

SAVY, JEAN
Discharged. See the roll dated at Calais May 2, 1763.

SCELLIER, CHARLES
Discharged March 31, 1761. See the roll of the same year, folio 36.

LOUISIANA TROOPS —:— 1720-1770

SCHELEGER, JOSEPH
Discharged February 6, 1770, with half-pay of 4 livres per month according to a decision of April 28, 1770.

SCHEMITT, HUBERT
Died at Caskakias, May 5, 1756, company of Favrot.

SCHEMITZ, ABRAHAM
Discharged November 16, 1769, roll of January 1, 1763, folio 49.

SCHENBERCK, MAURICE

SCHMITZ, ANTOINE
Discharged February 6, 1770, with half-pay of 6 livres per month according to a decision of April 27, 1751, sent to the Bureau des Invalides. Company of Vaugine.

SCHTORM, AUGUSTIN
Dismissed May 25, 1769, roll of January 1, 1763, folio 38.

SCOUDER, JACQUES
Discharged February 6, 1770, with half-pay of 4 livres 10 sols per month according to a decision of April 28, 1770.

SCOULIER, THOMAS
Discharged February 6, 1770, with half-pay of 4 livres 10 sols per month according to a decision of April 28, 1770. Company of Trudeau.

SCOUYER, THOMAS

SEGUIN, JEAN

SELLIER, TOUSSAINT

SENECHAL, JEAN GLAND
Died November 20, 1736.

SENECHAL, JEAN JOSEPH
Discharged March 31, 1761. See the roll of the same year folio 22.

SENECHAL, PIERRE

SENECAL or SENECHAL PIERRE
Discharged February 6, 1770. Company of Duplessis.

SEQUIN, JEAN

SERANO, THOMAS
Discharged November 30, 1769, roll of January 1, 1763, folio 41.

SERIGNOT, ANNE
Died February 13, 1746, company of Membrede.

SERINGE, NICOLAS

SERVILLE, MICHEL
Discharged February 1, 1764, roll of January 1, 1763, folio 30.

SERVIN, PIERRE

SERVRAISE, CLAUDE
Discharged September 15, 1763, roll of January 1, 1763, folio 16.

SERVRAISE, JOSEPH
Discharged September 15, 1763, roll of January 1, 1763, folio 17.

SETIER, PAUL
With half-pay of 6 ilvres per month according to a decision of April 4, 1764, sent to the Bureau des Invalides April 5, 1764. Discharged September 15, 1763.

SIEBERFING, MARTIN

SIBILLOT, MICHEL
Drowned in the sinking of the Pere de Famille February 17, 1770, returning to France.

SIBILOT, JEAN
Died at the hospital August 29, 1756, company of Macarty.

SIFFET, LOUIS
Condemned to the gallies June 3, 1750.

SIMANTE, GEORGES
Dismissed July 27, 1769, roll of January 1, 1763, folio 37.

SIMON, JEAN
Died at the hospital April 16, 1763, roll of January 1, 1763, folio 24.

SIMON, THOMAS

SIMONET, JOSEPH

SIMONET, JOSEPH
Discharged February 6, 1770, with half-pay of 4 livres 10 sols per month according to a decision of April 28, 1770.

SIMONNEAU, FRANCOIS
Deserted April 14, 1750.

SIRET, JEAN

LOUISIANA TROOPS —:— 1720-1770

SIROGUE, MARTIN
Discharged April 18, 1756, went to France.

SONSOIS, LOUIS
With half-pay of 12 livres per month according to a decision of November 30, 1764, sent to the Bureau des Invalides December 1, 1764. Discharged July 1, 1764. Sergeant, company of Murat.

SORIAUX, ANDRÉ
Died at the hospital at New Orleans March 7, 1761. See the roll of the same year folio 4.

SORIAUX, PIERRE

SORIN, LOUIS

SOUDAN, JOSEPH
Soldier. Company of Demazilieres. Deserted October 17, 1765. Condemned by contumacy following a judgement rendered in Louisiana October 17, 1765.

SOULARD, GABRIEL
Died October 25, 1754, company of Murat.

SOUILLOT, JEAN PIERRE

SOUILLOT, JEAN PIERRE
Drowned in the sinking of the Pere de Famille February 17, 1770, returning to France.

SOYARD, PIERRE
Died October 9, 1751.

SPEIGLE, ALEXANDRE
Discharged because of being an invalid, drummer, company of Grandpre.

STAULIVE or ST. AULIVE, NOEL
Died April 26, 1735.

STEIGRE, JOSEPH
Died November 29, 1750.

STUARD, GUILLEAUME ANDRÉ

SUISSER, PAUL
Died at the hospital November 3, 1754, company of De La Houssaye.

SUPPÉ, JEAN
Died at the hospital November 7, 1756, company of Gourdon.

SYLVESTRE, CLAUDE
With half-pay of 9 livres per month according to a decision of June 11, 1764, sent to the Bureau des Invalides June 12 1764.

LOUISIANA TROOPS —:— 1720-1770

TAGOT, JACQUES FRANCOIS
Discharged December 30, 1769, roll of January 1, 1763, folio 52.

TAILLANDIER, MICHEL
Drowned November 18, 1756, company of Benoist.

TAILLEFER, JEAN FRANCOIS

TAILLOU, JEAN
Discharged October 8, 1769, roll of January 1, 1763, folio 50.

TALON, JEAN JULIEN
Died at the hospital July 26, 1767, roll of January 1, 1763, folio 35.

TAMOINEAU, PIERRE
Deserted in Arkancas October 26, 1759. See the roll of June 1, 1760, folio 4.

TAMPIER, ETIENNE

TAQUEDA, PIERRE
Deserted April 27, 1751.

TARDIER, LOUIS
Discharged August 1, 1754.

TARDY, PIERRE
Corporal. Discharged February 6, 1770, with half-pay of 6 livres per month according to a decision of April 28, 1770.

TARDY, RENARD

TARDIVET, CHARLES

TRADIVET, CHARLES
Drowned in the sinking of the Pere de Famille February 17, 1770, returning to France.

TASSIN, PIERRE
Habitant since June 1, 1751.

TATTON, JEAN JULIEN

TAURICH, FAYE
Engaged in 1764. Discharged November 16, 1769, roll of January 1, 1763, folio 52

TAVERNIER, JEAN
Remained in Illinois. Roll of January 1, 1763, folio 38.

TASSEAU, JEAN JACQUES
Drowned November 28, 1751.

TELLIER, JEAN
Deserted August 30, 1761. See the roll of the same year, folio 43.

TENARD, FRANCOIS
Corporal. With half-pay of 8 livres per month according to a decision of April 4, 1764, sent to the Bureau des Invalides the same day.

TENDRE, JEAN
Drowned in the river October 2, 1754, company of Desmazellieres.

TERNIER, ETIENNE
Discharged September 15, 1763, roll of January 1, 1763, folio 4.

TERRENOIRE, JEAN JOSEPH
Discharged September 15, 1763, roll of January 1, 1763, folio 2.

TERRIER, PIERRE
Died September 6, 1751.

TESSIER, GABRIEL

TESSIER, GABRIEL

TESSIER, GABRIEL
Discharged February 6, 1770, company of Duplessis.

TESTOT, CLAUDE
With half-pay of 8 livres per month according to a decision of April 4, 1764, sent to the Bureau dts Invalides April 5, 1764.

TETARD, FRANCOIS

TEVENOT, JEAN
Sergeant. With half-pay of 10 livres per month according to a decision of April 4, 1764, sent to the Bureau des Invalides April 5, 1764.

TEXIER, JACQUES

TEXIER, PIERRE
Condemned to the gallies for life February 9, 1756, company of Aubry.

THERIAU, RAYMOND
Deserted August 1, 1750.

THERIS, MATHIEU
On extended leave in 1745, went to France.

THIBAULT, JEAN
Died February 28, 1751.

THIBAULT, NICOLAS
Discharged December 31, 1764, roll of January 1, 1763, folio 29.

LOUISIANA TROOPS —:— 1720-1770

THIBEAUDAU, MICHEL
Discharged September 15, 1763, roll of January 11, (?) 1763, folio 21.

THIERRE, NICOLAS
Discharged November 15, 1769, roll of January 1, 1763, folio 41.

THIERRY, LOUIS
Discharged September 15, 1763, roll of January 1, 1763, folio 1.

THIERS, FRANCOIS
With half-pay of 6 livres per month according to a decision of April 4, 1764, sent to the Bureau des Invalides April 5, 1764.

THIOT, GILLES
Discharged September 15, 1763, roll of January 1, 1763, folio 18.

THOMAS, PIERRE

THOMAS, RENÉ
Died at Natchez February 1, 1756, company of Gourdon.

THOMASSIN, ANTOINE

THOUIN, RENÉ
Discharged July 16, 1756, went to France.

THULLIER, ADRIEN
Died September 1, 1735.

TIERCELIN, PHILIPPE JOSEPH
Died July 31, 1751.

TIMON, NIZIER
Discharged August 18, 1751.

TINON, CLAUDE

TIRQUIT, ANTOINE
Died April 4, 1761. See the roll of the same year, folio 46.

TISON, ANTOINE
Executed by the firing squad July 14, 1745, for (taking part in a) rebellion. Company of Marest.

TISSERAND, JOSEPH
Died September 14, 1751.

TIESSET, LOUIS
Discharged November 1, 1756.

TIXERAND, GERARD
Deserted in June 1759. See the roll of June 1, 1760, folio 4.

TOFFIN, PIERRE
Died at the hospital August 4, 1757, company of Trant.

TON, PIERRE
Died at the hospital February 25, 1754, company of Gourdon.

TOREL, MICHEL

TOREL, MICHEL
Discharged November 16, 1769, roll of January 1, 1763, folio 52.

TORTILLÉ, JACQUES
Died August 20, 1751.

TOUCHARD, JEAN
With half-pay of 6 livres per month according to a decision of April 4, 1764, sent to the Bureau des Invalides.

TOUCHÉE, PIERRE

TOURBEIR, FRANCOIS
With half-pay of 9 livres per month according to a decision of April 4, 1764, sent to the Bureau des Invalides April 5, 1764. Discharged September 15, 1763.

TOURNIER, GUILLAUME
Died at the hospital May 13, 1756, company of Montberault.

TOURNIER, JEAN

TOURTILLÉ, JACQUES

TOUSEL, ETIENNE JOSEPH
Died August 29, 1751.

TOUTIN, CHARLES
Discharged November 1, 1750.

TOUVENEL, ROBERT
Deserted June 8, 1756.

TOUZÉ, LOUIS
Died at Natchez October 6, 1754, company of Chabert.

TRANCHA, ALEXIS
Died October 11, 1734.

TRAPÉ, MICHEL

TRAVAUX, LOUIS CHARLES
Died September 16, 1754, company of Orgon.

TRAVERS, THOMAS
Deserted February 5, 1739.

TREVILLE, FRANCOIS
Killed or taken by the Cherakis or Chiachai November 9, 1757, company of Sommes.

TRIBOULET, JEAN
Deserted March 15, 1746.

LOUISIANA TROOPS —:— 1720-1770

TRISTAN, PIERRE
Condemned by contumacy for desertion. See the proceedings of September 30, 1753.

TRONCY, BENOIST

TRONQUET, PIERRE
Discharged August 16, 1756.

TRUCHET, FRANCOIS

TRUCHON, DENIS FRANCOIS

TRUDEAU, ROSALIE

TRUDEL, JEAN ETIENNE
Discharged December 14, 1754.

TRUFFLOT, LOUIS JACQUES
Discharged September 15, 1763 roll of January 1, 1763, folio 16.

TUAL, GUILLAUME
Fusileer. With half-pay of 6 livres per month payable at Dol in Britanny, according to a decision of September 8, 1770, and sent to the Bureau des Invalides September 14, 1770.

TUAL, GUILLAUME ANDREA

TUAL, GUILLAUME ANDREA
Invalid soldier. Discharged September 15, 1763, roll of January 1, 1763, folio 4, Drowned in the sinking of the Pere de Famille February 17, 1770, returning to France.

TUDEAU, FRANCOIS
Discharged November 30, 1768. He served twenty one years with half-pay of 7 livres 10 sols per month according to a decision of June 2, 1769.

TUMERMAN, JOSEPH
Discharged September 1, 1751.

TURION, FRANCOIS
Died December 28, 1751.

TURPOT, JACQUES
Discharged November 15, 1769, roll of January 1, 1763, folio 40.

TUYAU, PIERRE NICOAS
Deserted or lost toward the end of April, 1755, company of La Gautraye.

LOUISIANA TROOPS —:— 1720-1770

VACHÉ, ANTOINE

VACHELIER, GILBERT
Died October 15, 1751.

VACHEZ, ANTOINE
Discharged February 6, 1770, with half-pay of 6 livres per month according to a decision of April 28, 1770.

VAILLANT, LOUIS NICOLAS
Died at the hospital June 9, 1767, roll of January 1, 1763, folio 35.

VALIS, ANTOINE
Died at the hospital November 25, 1768, roll of January 1, 1763, folio 36.

VALLÉ, MAURICE

VALLY, ANDRÉ
Died February 20, 1751.

VARÉ, FRANCOIS
Executed by the firing squad February 9, 1756, company of Neyon.

VARETTE, HENRY

VASCOCU, ANTOINE
Discharged September 15, 1763, roll of January 1, 1763, folio 6.

VASPY, ANTOINE
Deserted at (the post of) Alibamons January 15, 1755.

VASSERON, BERNARD JOSEPH

VASSERON, BERNARD JOSEPH
Discharged February 6, 1770. Company of Villiers.

VATONNE, BARTHELEMY
Discharged September 15, 1763, roll of January 1, 1763, folio 17.

VAUDOIS, NICOLAS

VAUQUIRE, ELOY

VAUQUIERE, ELOY
Died at the hospital July 19 1755, company of Grandpre.

VERDELLE, FRANCOIS LOUIS

VERDET, JOSEPH
Drowned in the sinking of the Pere de Famille February 17, 1770, returning to France.

VERDETTE, FRANCOIS

VERDIER, PIERRE
Sergeant. Drowned in the sinking of the Pere de Famille February 17, 1770, returning to France.

VERGERONT, FRANCOIS
Drowned at Ouabache November 10, 1756, company of Mazan.

VERGNON, GABRIEL
Deserted at Campeche in 1755 or 1756.

VERNON, JOSEPH THOMAS
Discharged for France (sic) July 10, 1756.

VEROUIL, NICOLAS
Died at the hospital March 19, 1757, company of Bellenos.

VERRIER, ETIENNE
Drowned returning from the (post of the) Alibamons October 1, 1759. See the roll of June 1, 1760, folio 2.

VERRON, ETIENNE

VERRON, FRANCOIS
Went to France on the Samson October 1, 1769, roll of January 1, 1763, folio 5.

VERSIAU, ANDRÉ
Died September 27, 1738. The death certificate is in the bureau in proper form.

VEVRES, PHILIPES ADAM
Discharged July 1, 1750.

VHAUD, JEAN
Discharged July 10, 1754, and returned to France on the Rhinoceros.

VIAL, JOSEPH MARIE
With half-pay of 9 livres per month according to a decision of May 25, 1764, sent to the Bureau des Invalides. Discharged September 15, 1763, roll of January 1' 1763, folio 2.

VIALA, FRANCOIS
Died October 1, 1751.

VIALAUD, PIERRE
Discharged November 16, 1769, roll of January 1, 1763, folio 48.

LOUISIANA TROOPS —:— 1720-1770

VIART, LAURENT FRANCOIS
Discharged September 15, 1763, roll of January 1 1763, folio 14.

VIDAL, PASCAL
Condemned to the gallies May 6, 1751.

VIDOUX, FRANCOIS
Discharged September 15, 1763, roll of January 1, 1763, folio 14.

VIÉ, ANTOINE
Died August 25, 1751.

VIEL, ANTOINE
Discharged February 6, 1770, company of Duplessis.

VIET, FRANCOIS
Discharged September 15, 1763, roll of January 1, 1763, folio 24.

VIEUX, PIERRE
Discharged September 15, 1763, roll of January 1, 1763, folio 5.

VIGNON, JEAN RENÉ
Discharged August 10, 1754.

VIGOUREUX, CORNIL JOSEPH
Executed by the firing squad June 16, 1751.

VIGROUX, CHARLES PHILIPPES
Discharged by court order in 1754.

VIGUEROUX, CHARLES

VILCAIN, JEAN FRANCOIS
Discharged. See the roll dated at Calais May 2, 1763.

VILLANES, JEAN FRANCOIS
Discharged February 6, 1770, with half-pay of 4 livres 10 sols per month according to a decision of April 28, 1770.

VILLERET, JEAN MARTIN
Discharged September 1, 1764, with half-pay of 6 livres per month according to a decision of September 8, 1770.

VILLERET, JEAN MIN.
With half-pay of 6 livres per month payable at Bezancon according to a decision of September 8, 1770, sent to the Bureau des Invalides September 14, 1770.

VILLEROUX, FRANCOIS
Died November 6, 1750.

VILLET, FRANCOIS

VILLOT, FRANCOIS
Canonier Bombardiers. Drowned in the sinking of the Pere de Famille February 17, 1770, returning to France.

VILLIERES, CLAUDE
Discharged and went to France on the Rhinoceros April 18, 1756.

VILMANE, JACQUES
Died February 11, 1745, company of Gauvry.

VILMENAYE, JOSEPH
Died at Natchez in 1745 or 1746.

VINCENT, AUGUSTIN NICOLAS
Engaged March 16, 1769. Discharged October 8, 1769, roll of January 1, 1763, folio 55.

VINCENT, JEAN
Discharged September 15, 1763. Roll of January 1, 1763, folio 22.

VINCENT, PIERRE
Drowned December 30, 1751.

VINDOS, HENRY
Drowned November 20, 1750.

VINET, FRANCOIS
Discharged February 16, 1764, roll of January 1, 1763, folio 27.

VIOLLON, PIERRE
Discharged February 6, 1770, with half-pay of 4 livres 10 sols per month according to a decision of April 28, 1770.

VIOLON, PIERRE
Discharged February 1, 1751. Re-engaged.

VIRARD, PIERRE

VIRAUVAUCOURT, PIERRE
Died October 6, 1751.

VITCOQ, PIERRE
  Died October 31, 1751.

VITER, PIERRE
  Discharged August 1, 1766, roll of January 1, 1763, folio 33.

VITREQUIN, GATIEN
  Discharged April 1, 1750.

VIVIEN, LOUIS

VIVIER, FRANCOIS

VOIGNIER, JEAN
  Sergeant. With half-pay of 12 livres per month according to a decision of April 4, 1764, sent to the Bureau des Invalides April 5, 1764. Discharged September 15, 1763.

VOISEAU, CLAUDE FRANCOIS

VOISIN, JEAN PIERRE
  Died at the hospital November 9, 1765, roll of January 1, 1765, folio 31.

VOLTRE, MATHIEU

VTOIS, DANIEL
  Discharged February 6, 1770. Company of Duplessis.

LOUISIANA TROOPS —:— 1720-1770

WILLAUME, ANTOINE
WOUA, JEAN
Died at the hospital August 29, 1757, company of Trant.
WOURNE, JOSEPH
Discharged September 15, 1763, roll of January 1, 1763, folio 14.

WOURNE, JOSEPH
With half-pay of 6 livres per month according to a decision of April 4, 1764, sent to the Bureau des Invalides April 5, 1764.

LOUISIANA TROOPS —:— 1720-1770

YENTZEN, GUIBERT   YOU, SIMON

LOUISIANA TROOPS —:— 1720-1770

ZIZANY, FRANCOIS
   Died October 27, 1751.

LOUISIANA OFFICERS
1692 - 1776

ACHART
Second lieutenant, 15 May 1762.

ADAM
Lieutenant in the batallion of St. Lo; ensign in Louisiana, 1 October 1750; lieutenant, 1 July 1759.

AMELOT
Lieutenant in the Regiment of Grassin; captain in Louisiana, 1 October 1750; engineer, 15 October 1752; Chevalier de St. Louis, 1 August 1759.

ANDRY
Lieutenant reformé, sub-engineer, 18 June 1762.

ARTAUD
He served five years in the capacity of volunteer in the Regiment du meotre de Camp general, according to a certificate of the Duke de Chaulnes Cornette in 1746; lieutenant of the Regiment of La Morliere, 16 July 1747; captain in Louisiana, 1 July 1751; Chevalier de St. Louis, 16 May 1762. He returned to France in retirement due to poor health, but being fully recovered after the rest here (in France), and asking to return to Louisana, Monseigneur wrote, 16 May 1762, to M. de Kerlerec, governor of that colony, to reappoint him to the head of a company, or to give him a commandancy o fa post. Nota: In the month of July, 1770, he was accorded a raise of 400 livres pension, which carried his reformé to 800 livres.

AUBERT
Lieutenant in Grassin, 1747; lieutenant in Louisana, 1 October 1750; aide-major of Mobile, 15 October 1752; captain, 1 July 1759; Chevalier de St. Louis, 1 September 1774. He has a pension of 800 livres from the colonial funds, by a decision in 1774.

AUBERT
Lieutenant in the Regiment of Grassin; lieutenant in Louisiana, 1750; aide-major at Mobile, 1752; captain en pied, 1 July 1759.

AUBRY
Lieutenant in the Regiment of Lyonnais Infantry, 1742; captain in Louisiana, 1 October 1750; Chevalier de St .Louis, 10 July 1761.

BAILLEUL CANUT
Second lieutenant in Canada, 15 April 1750; ensign en pied in Canada, 15 March 1755; lieutenant in Canada, 1 January 1759; Chevalier de St. Louis, 24 March 1761; went to Louisiana in the same capacity by an order of 1 January 1762. He was not able to reach his destination, having been taken (prisoner?) in route and returned to Rochefort. Retired with a pension of 600 livres from the colonial funds, beginning from 1 February 1767.

BAUDIN
Second lieutenant, 15 October 1752; ensign en pied, 1 July 1759; 100 livres increase on his reformé pension of 200 livres from 1 January 1766.

BEAURANS
Second lieutenant at Isle Royalle, 15 April 1750; ensign en pied in Louisiana, 1 January 1756.

BERNARD D'AUTERIVE
Second lieutenant of the Royal Volunteers, 16 April 1748; reformé in 1749; lieutenant in Louisiana, 1 October 1750; captain, 22 March 1755.

BERNAUDY
Second lieutenant, 1 October 1762.

BOBÉ DESCLOZEAU, JR.
Scrivener-ordinary, acting as comptroller of Louisiana by an order of 15 May 1765.

BOBÉ DES CLOZEAUX
Commissioner of the Marine; Ordonnateur, 1 August 1759. He was retired in January, 1762, with 2000 livres pension from the funds of the Invalides de la Marine. The order of ordonnateur dispatched to him 1 August 1759, was never executed. The order for retirement was dispatched to the bureau of officers.

BOISSEAU
Second lieutenant, 1 December 1747; ensign en pied, 1 February, 1754; lieutenant, 1 July 1759.

BOULANGER
Lieutenant of the grenadiers in the batallion of Peronne; ensign in Louisiana, 1 October 1750; lieutenant, 1 October 1762.

BROSSARD
Cadet a l'aiguillette, 1756; second lieutenant, 1 January 1762.

BROUTIN
Second lieutenant, 15 October 1752; M. de Kerlerec accorded him permission to return to France and the letter of this governor, dated 12 July 1761, says that he will be a very bad subject ... in the colony.

BOULANGER
Lieutenant of the grenadiers in the batallion of Peronne; ensign in Louisiana, 1 October, 1750; lieutenant, 1 October 1762.

BUCHET
Principal scrivener; dead.

C

CABARET d'ETRÉPIS
Lieutenant, 1 February 1754; captain, 1 October 1762; Chevalier de St. Louis, 15 August 1771.

CABARET d'ETREPY
Lieutenant, 1 February 1754; captain, 1 October 1762.

CARLIER
Scrivener-ordinary, acting as comptroller by an order of 20 May 1759.

CHABERT
Lieutenant in the Royal Infantry Regiment, 1747; captain in Louisana, 1 July 1751; Chevalier de St .Louis, 4 March 1776.

CHANTALOU
Recorder of the Council. Nota: The provisions for recorder of the council were dispatched to Sieur Garic, hereafter named.

CHAUVET DUBREUIL
Ensign en pied, 1 January 1762.

CHAUVIN
Second lieutenant, 1 October 1762.

CHEVALIER D'ERNEVILLE
Second lieutenant, 1732; ensign en pied, 1733; lieutenant, 18 July 1734; Captain, 1 October 1740; Chevalier de St. Louis, 1 February 1754. He was recalled by an order of 1 October 1759, to be sent back to France. Mgr. remarked on the 18 January 1762, to Mr. de Kerlerec, governor of Louisiana, that the King left it to him to execute the order or to retain it, according to what seemed proper to him. An order of 24 April 1769, reestablished the Chevalier d'Erneville . . . (also) a pension . . . of 1080 livres in appointment which he enjoys as a captain, and furthermore, he was accorded an extraordinary gratuity of 1200 livres.

CHEVALIER de CLOUET
Served fourteen years in the Regiment of Egmont dragoons; lieutenant in Louisiana, 20 February 1758.

CHEVALIER de GLAPPION
Second lieutenant, 1 February 1754; ensign en pied, 1 July 1759.

CHEVALIER de LIGNERIS
Cadet a l'aiguillette in Canada; second lieutenant in Louisiana, 1 July 1762.

CHEVALIER de LUSSER
Second lieutenant, 1 June 1746; ensign en pied, 15 October 1752; lieutenant, 1 July 1759.

CHEVALIER de MACARTY
Sub-lieutenant in France; second lieutenant in Louisiana 1736; lieutenant, 1 October 1741; captain, 1 February 1754.

CHEVALIER de NOYAN (CHAVOY)
Officer in the service of the Company (of the Indies); ensign at Isle Royale, 8 May 1730; lieutenant in Louisiana 20 September 1735; aide-major at Mobile, 15 October 1736; captain, 1 October 1740; captain en pied, 1 January 1744; Chevalier de St. Louis, 15 October 1752.

CHEVALIER de ROCHEBLAVE
Second lieutenant, 1752; ensign en pied, 1 July 1759. Put in prison by order of the governor and should not be released except to be sent back to France. See the letter of M. de Kerlerec of 30 March 1760.

CHEVALIER de ROUVILLE
Second lieutenant, 1 June 1746; ensign en pied, 11 June 1750; lieutenant, 1 July 1759.

CHEVALIER de VELLE
Musketeer; lieutenant in Louisiana, 17 August 1732; captain, 15 October 1736; aide-major at Mobile, 1 January 1744; Chevalier de St. Louis, 11 June 1750; major at Mobile, 15 October 1752; lieutenant of the King at Mobile, 1 July 1759.

CHEVALIER de VILLIERS (RICARD)
Second lieutenant, 15 October 1725; ensign en pied, 1 February 1754; lieutenant, 1 July 1759.

CHEVALIER de VILLIERS
Ensign, 15 October 1736; lieutenant, 1 June 1746; captain, 1 February 1754; Chevalier de St. Louis, 1 August 1759.

COULON de VILLIERS
Second lieutenant, 15 May 1762.

CHEVALIER de LA HOUSSAYE
Served in the French Guards, the Regiment of Vintinielle, and in the Coast Guards of Aunis; Chevalier de St. Louis; captain in Louisiana, 1 October 1750; Major at Mobile, 1 July 1759.

CHEVALIER de LA RONDE
Second lieutenant, 1 June 1746; ensign en pied, 11 June 1750; lieutenant, 1 July 1759.

CHEVALIER DESSALLES
Lieutenant, 1 July 1759; cadet a l'Eguillette, 6 December 1759.

CHEVALIER DU FOSSAT
Lieutenant in the Regiment of Monaco, 1747; lieutenant in Louisiana, 1 October 1750; captain, 1 July 1759.

COPPIN
Second lieutenant in France, 1745; ensign in Louisiana, 7 October 1750; lieutenant, 1 February 1754; captain, 1 October 1762; Chevalier de St. Louis, 1 January 1773.

COPPIN
Second lieutenant in France, 1745; ensign in Louisiana, 1 October 1750; lieutenant, 1 February 1754; captain, 1 October 1762.

D'ABBADIE
Commissioner of the Marine; Commissioner - General; Ordonnateur in Louisiana, 29 December 1761. Dead.

DE BACHEMIN
Second lieutenant, 15 October, 1752; ensign en pied, 1 July 1759.

de BELLEISLE
Ensign en pied, 1 February 1754.

DE BELLENOS
Served fourteen years in the regiment of the Swiss Guards; lieutenant of grenadiers in the Regiment of Louvendal, 1744; captain in the militia batallion of Dman (sic), 1748; captain in Santo Domingo, 1 October 1750; went to Louisiana as captain by an order of 1 January 1758; Chevalier de St. Louis, 16 May 1762.

DE BELLISLE
Second lieutenant, 1 December 1747; ensign en pied, 1 February 1754; lieutenant, 1 July 1759.

de BERQUEVILLE
Second lieutenant, 15 May 1762.

DE BLANC
Captain in the service of the Company (of the Indies), cashiered by the said company and made captain, 18 July 1734; commmandant at Natchitoches, 1746; Chevalier de St. Louis, 11 June 1750.

DE BONNILLE
Ensign, 1728; lieutenant, 14 September 1735; captain, 11 June 1750; Chevalier de St. Louis, 1 August 1759.

DE BONREPOS
King's page; second lieutenant, 15 October 1752; ensign en pied, 1 February 1754.

de BREMOND
Cadet a l'aiguillette, 1758 second lieutenant, 1 January 1762.

de BRESSAY
Ensign bearer in the Regiment of Brancas, cavalry, 3 April 1746; lieutenant of the same regiment, 20 July following. The last two statements are verified in the Bureau, 19 June 1770. He was reformé 21 November 1748; lieutenant for recruits at Isle of Ré 1 November 1751; captain of the colonial troops serving at the Isle of Ré, 28 September 1757; captain at Santo Domingo, 1 November 1761; went to Louisiana by an order of 31 December 1761. (He) is (now) major of the Regiment of recruits of the colony at Isle of Ré.

de CHABRILLARD
Lieutenant reformé in France; lieutenant in Louisana, 1 July 1751; captain, 1 January 1762.

DE CHABRILLARD
Lieutenant reformé; lieutenant in Louisiana, 1751; captain, 1 January 1762.

DE CHATEAUBODAU
Ensign en pied, 1 April 1758.

de CHEVENNES
Second lieutenant, 15 May 1762.

de CIRCE
Second lieutenant, 15 May 1762; died at sea on board the Thetis, returning to France, 4 June 1770. The death certificate is placed in the Louisiana package.

DE COURT DE PRESLES
Second lieutenant, 11 June 1750; ensign en pied, 1 February 1754.

DE FONTENELLE
Lieutenant of the grenadiers in the batallion of Poitiers, 1747; ensign in Louisiana, 1 October 1750; lieutenant, 1 October 1762.

DE FOURCROY
Lieutenant in the Regiment of Orleans; Infantry; lieutenant in Louisiana, 1751; quit and returned to France, 175__.

de GENTILLY
Second lieutenant, 15 May 1762.

DE GRANDMAISON
Ensign bearer of the cavalry in Graissin, 1745; lieutenant in Louisana, 1 October 1750; captain, 1 February 1754; Chevalier de St. Louis, 23 December 1762; major of New Orleans, 16 March 1763.

DE GRANDPRÉ
Ensign, 1732: lieutenant, 1736; captain, 1741; Chevalier de St. Louis, 1 February 1754; He died in Louisiana 1 July 1763, as noted by Mr. de Kerlerec, governor, the fourth (day) of the same month and year.

DE GRUY
Second lieutenant, 1740; ensign en pied, 1746; lieutenant, 1752; captain, 1759. He died in 1759.

de JUZAN
Second lieutenant, 15 October 1752; ensign en pied, 15 May 1762.

de KERLEREC
Ensign en pied, 1 January 1762.

DE L'HOMMER
Lieutenant in the Regiment of Saxe Allemande, Infantry, 1747; lieutenant in Louisiana, 1 October 1750; captain, 1 July 1759.

de LA GAUTRAIS
Second lieutenant, 15 May 1762.

DE LA GROUE
Principal scrivener of the Marine, acting as comptroller, by an order of 22 October 1758.

DE LA LANDE
Councilor, 10 January 1762.

DE LA NOUE BOGARD
Ensign of the infantry in the Regiment of Bresse, 27 May 1743; lieutenant in the same regiment, 4 February 1744; reformé at the end of 1748; second lieutenant at Isle Royalle, 15 April 1750; ensign en pied at the same place, 1 April 1754; lieutenant in Louisiana, 20 February 1758; Chevalier de St. Louis 22 June 1771.

de LA PERRIÈRE
Lieutenant in the Regiment of Montboissier, King's guard, 1749; lieutenant in Louisiana, 1751; captain in Santo Domingo, 1 April 1762; captain in Louisiana, 1763; Chevalier de St. Louis, 19 March 1763.

DE LA TOUCHE
Second lieutenant, 1754; ensign en pied, 1 July 1759.

DE LA VERGNE
Lieutenant reformé, 1 December 1738; captain reformé, 1 December 1747; Chevalier de St. Louis, 1 August 1759.

DE LANTAGNAC
Ensign en pied, 1 July 1759.

de LAURE
Second lieutenant, 15 May 1762.

DE LAVAU
Second lieutenant, 15 October 1752; ensign en pied, 1 July 1759; brevet of captain in the colonial troops, 11 October 1774; Chevalier de St. Louis, 15 December 1776.

de LIGNERIES
Second lieutenant in Canada, 1 May 1757; ensign en pied in Canada, 1 February 1760; went to Louisiana by an order of 1 June 1762.

DE LIVAUDAIS
Port captain at New Orleans with a brevet of captain de flute, 18 July 1734; Chevalier de St. Louis, 1 August 1759.

DE LIVAUDAIS, THE ELDER
Second lieutenant, 15 October 1752; ensign en pied, 1 February 1754; lieutenant, 1 July 1759.

de LONGUEVAL
Second lieutenant, 15 May 1762.

DE LORRY
Lieutenant, 1 February 1754.

DE LUSSER
Second lieutenant, 15 October 1736; ensign en pied, 1 October 1740; lieutenant, 1 December 1747; captain, 1 July 1759.

DE MACARTY
Musketeer, aide-major, 1732; captain, 14 September 1735; Chevalier de St. Louis. 16 July 1750; major in Illinois, 11 June 1750; lieutenant of the King at New Orleans, 1 July 1759. Died 20 April 1764 (according to) Aubry ...

DE MANDEVILLE
Second lieutenant, 1 October 1740; ensign en pied, I June 1746; lieutenant, 15 October 1752.

DE MEZIERES
Cadet a l'aiguillette; expectative of second lieutenant, 1 December 1748; lieutenant reformé, 1 April 1749; captain reformé, 1 February 1754; Chevalier de St. Louis, 4 August 1772.

DE MONCHERVAUX
Ensign, 1732; Lieutenant, 15 October 1736; captain, 1 December 1747.

de MONTCHERVAUX, JR.
Second lieutenant, 15 May 1762.

DE MONTBERAULT
Lieutenant reformé, 1 September 1738; lieutenant en pied, 1 January 1744; captain reformé, 1 June 1749; captain en pied, 1 October 1750 (?); Chevalier de St. Louis, 28 June 1771. (His full name is) Henry Elizabeth Aimé de Montault (sic), retired; see the letter of M. de Kerlerec of 25 January 1762. (He) obtained a pension of 400 livres on 1 August 1769.

de MONTBERAULT, THE ELDER
Cadet a l'Eguillette, 1 August 1753. (Under this name is listed:) Louis Augustin de Montault, age twenty-three in 1770; second lieutenant, 15 May 1762.

DE MONTREUIL
Second lieutenant, 1 October 1740; ensign en pied, 1 June 1746; lieutenant, 1 February 1754.

DE MOUY
Second lieutenant, 1 February 1754; ensign en pied, 15 May 1762.

de MOUY
Second lieutenant, 1 February 1758; ensign en pied, 15 May 1762.

DE MURAT
Lieutenant, was eight years in the Regiment of La Tour of Auvergne; captain in Louisiana, 1 October 1750; retired See the letter of M. de Kerlerec of 1 September 1758, no. 152, and that of the said day attached, unnumbered.

DE NANTOUILLET
Lieutenant, 1 October 1750.

de NESLE
Lieutenant of the cavalry of the de Fiennes Regiment; lieutenant for recruitment at the Isle of Ré, 28 September 1757; went to Santo Domingo, 1 November 1761; went to Louisiana by an order of 31 December 1761.

DE NEYON de VILLIERS
Ensign in the Choiseul regiment, 1735; reformé in 1738; lieutenant in the regiment of Merinville, 1742; aide-major of the regiment of Lorraine, 1744; captain of the regiment of Lorraine, 1747; reformé in 1748; captain in Louisiana, 1750; major-commandant at Illinois, 1 July 1759; Chevalier de St. Louis, 1 August 1759.

DE NOYAN
Ensign en pied, 1752; lieutenant, 1759; retired by an order of 6 July 1760.

DE PORTNEUF
Second lieutenant; ensign en pied, 1 October 1740; lieutenant, 11 June 1750; captain, 1 July 1759.

DE REGGIO
Lieutenant with a commission of captain in the Royal Genoese Grenadiers, 1748; captain in Louisiana, 1 October 1750.

DE ROCHE de BEAUMONT
Officer reformé of Lancize; ensign in Louisiana, 1 October 1750.

DE ROCHEBLAVE
Lieutenant in France, 1748; lieutenant in Louisiana, 1 December 1752.

DE ROCHEMORE
General commissioner of the Marine; ordonnateur, 1 August 1757; recalled to France by an order of 1 August 1759. He was dispatched by new orders for his recall 29 December 1761.

DE SANTILLY
Second lieutenant, 1 September 1738; ensign en pied, 1 January 1744; lieutenant, 15 October 1752; captain, 1 October 1762.

de SANTILLY
Second lieutenant, 1 September 1738; ensign en pied, 1 January 1744; lieutenant, 15 October 1752; Chevalier de St. Louis, 21 September 1775.

DE SOIZY
Ensign en pied, 1 July 1759.

DE SOMME DE MONTY
Lieutenant in Raugrade, 1743; lieutenant in Louisiana, 1750; captain, 1754; retired and entered the Troupes Legeres in France.

DE TRANT
Ensign in the Regiment of Louvendal, 1744; second lieutenant in the same regiment, 1745; captain in Louisiana, 1 October 1750.

de TREMILLEC
Ensign en pied, 15 May 1762.

DE VAUCORET
Ensign en pied, 1 February 1759.

de VAUGINE de NUISMAN
Cadet in the Royal Artillary, 5 July 1744; lieutenant in the Royal German Bavarian Regiment, 15 April 1746; lieutenant in Louisiana, 1 October 1750; captain, 16 May 1763. The service record of de Vaugine de Nuisman also apeared first in this list, exactly as recorded above, obviously a duplication in one of the lists.

DE VELLE
Second lieutenant, 1 February 1754; ensign en pied, 1 July 1759.

DE VERGEZ
Engineer at New Orleans; Chevalier de St. Louis, 15 October 1752.

DE VILEMONT
Captain reformé in the Regiment of Ferrary, 1745; captain en pied in the same regiment, 1747; captain in Louisiana, 1750; Chevalier de St. Louis, 8 February 1761; lieutenant-colonel of the cavalry, (no date). (He) went into the service of Canada by an order of 1 February 1760; an order of the King permitted him to join the service of the King of Spain from 13 December 1763.

de VILLEBOEUVE
Second lieutenant, 15 May 1762.

de VILLIERS, THE ELDER
Second lieutenant, 15 May 1762.

DE VIN
Second lieutenant, 15 October 1752; ensign en pied, 1 July 1759.

de VOLSEY
Officer reformé of Lancize; ensign in Louisiana, 1 October 1750; lieutenant, 1 October 1762; captain, 21 September 1775; Chevalier de St. Louis, 21 September 1775.

de VOLSEY
Officer reformé of Lancize; ensign in Louisiana, 1 October 1750; lieutenant, 1 October 1762.

DU BARRY
Second lieutenant in the Regiment de la Couronne, 10 June 1743; lieutenant in the same regiment, 9 December 1745; reformé in 1749 with 150 livres pension; lieutenant in Louisiana, 1 July 1751; aide-major at Mobile with a commission of captain, 1 July 1759; Chevalier de St. Louis, 1 July 1770.

DU CLOS
Second lieutenant, 1 December 1740; ensign en pied, 1 February 1754.

DU CODER
Second lieutenant, 8 September 1733; ensign en pied, 1 October 1740; lieutenant, 1 June 1746.

DU TILLET
Ensign in the Regiment of Foix, 1747; captain in Louisiana, 1 October 1750.

DU TISNÉ, THE ELDER
Second lieutenant, 15 October 1752; ensign en pied, 1 February 1754; lieutenant, 1 October 1762.

DU TISNEZ, THE CADET
Second lieutenant, 1 February 1754; ensign en pied, 1 July 1759.

DU TISNEZ, THE ELDER
Second lieutenant, 15 October 1752; ensign en pied, 1 February 1754; lieutenant, 1 October 1762.

DU VERGEZ SOUBADON
Second lieutenant, 1 February 1754; ensign en pied, 1 July 1759.

DU VERGEZ, THE ELDER
Second lieutenant, 15 October 1752; ensign en pied, 1 July 1759.

DES COUDREAUX (RENARD)
Second lieutenant, 1752; ensign en pied, 1754; lieutenant of the company of canoneers, 1 November 1759.

DES ILLETS DU MANOIR
Second lieutenant, 1 January 1762.

DES MAZELLIERES
Captain en second in the corps of the chasseurs of Colonne, 1747; captain in Louisiana, 1 October 1750.
Captain of the militia of Dauphiné, 1747; captain in Louisiana, 1 October 1750; Chevalier de St. Louis, 1 August 1759.

DARENSBOURG
Captain reformé, 1732; Chevalier de St. Louis, 1 August 1759.

DARENSBOURG, THE CADET
Second lieutenant, 1 February 1754; ensign en pied, 1 July 1759.

DARENSBOURG, THE ELDER
Second lieutenant, 15 October 1752; ensign en pied, 1 July 1759.

DAUTHERIVE DESVALLIERS
Cadet a l'aiguillette, 1 April 1755; second lieutenant, 1 January 1762.

DAUTHERIVE DUBUCLET
Cadet a l'aiguillette, 1 April 1755; second lieutenant, 1 January 1762.

DELFAU de PONTALBA
Second lieutenant, 1732; ensign en pied, 1735; lieutenant, 1740; captain, 1750; Chevalier de St. Louis, 1 August 1759; retired in 1759.

DENOIS
Second lieutenant, 1 January 1762; sub-lieutenant in the legion of the Isle de France.

DESPALIÈRES
Second lieutenant, 15 May 1762.

DESSALLES
Lieutenant reformé charged with the detail of the artillary, 1752; captain of the company of the Canoniers Bombardiers in Louisiana, 1 November 1759.

DESSALLES
Naval guard, 19 September 1749; pavillion guard, 17 January 1750; lieutenant reformé responsible for the detail of the artillary, 15 October 1752; captain-commandant of the company of cannoneers, 1 November 1759; rank and seniority of captain of the infantry from 1 January 1759 by an order of 8 December 1759; Chevalier de St. Louis, 18 January 1762. 400 livres of reformé in 1763 and 600 livres pension sur les Invalides de la marine, 1771.

DORIOCOURT
Second lieutenant of the militia in the batallion of St. Dizier, 1743; lieutenant in the same batallion, 28 December 1745; porte-drapeau in the Regiment of Grenadier Daulan, 30 April 1748; lieutenant of grenadiers in the batallion of St. Dizier, 10 March 1750; ensign in Louisiana, 1 October 1750; lieutenant, 1 July 1759; Chevalier de St. Louis, 15 August 1771.

DORVILLE
Captain, aide-major of the Regiment of Grassin; captain in Louisiana, 1 October 1750; aide-major of New Orleans, 1 February 1754.

DUBREUIL
Cadet a l'Eguillette, 1 March 1753; second lieutenant, 1 October 1762.

DOUIN DE LA MOTTE
Lieutenant, 1758. He was made captain at Santo Domingo, 20 April 1762. On 1 July 1759, he was granted an order which changed his destination, and which permitted him to stay in service at Martinique where he had been ill while going to Louisiana.

DUCLOS
Second lieutenant, 15 May 1762.

DUBREUIL ST. CYR
Second lieutenant, 15 May 1762.

DUPLESSIS
Ensign, 1738; ensign en pied, 1 October 1741; lieutenant, 11 June 1750; captain, 25 August 1758; Chevalier de St. Louis, 18 January 1762.

DUSSEAU
Ensign en pied, 1 October 1750; lieutenant, 1 July 1759.

DUVERGER ST. LUC
Second lieutenant, 15 May 1762.

DUVERGER ST. SAUVEUR
Second lieutenant, 1 October 1762.

E

ENOULD de LIVAUDAIS
Second lieutenant, 1 February 1754; ensign en pied, 1 July 1759.

FAGOT
Second lieutenant, 15 May 1762.

FAVROT
Ensign, 1732; lieutenant, 15 October 1736; captain, 11 June 1750; Chevalier de St. Louis, 1 August 1759. He had a 200 livres augmentation of pension to that of 400 livres of reformé, by a decision of 23 August 1759.

FAVROT
Second lieutenant, 1 October 1762; made first lieutenant in the regiment of America, 30 July 1773.

FAZENDE
Second lieutenant, 1 February 1754; ensign en pied, 1 October 1762.

FAZENDE
Scrivener-ordinary.

FERRAND
Second lieutenant, 15 October 1762; ensign en pied, 1 February 1754.

FLEURIAU
Expectve. de Lieutenant, 1 January 1748; lieutenant en pied, 11 June 1750; captain, 1 July 1759.

FONTENELLE
Lieutenant of the grenadiers in the batallion of Poitiers, 1747; ensign in Louisiana, 1 October 1750; lieutenant, 1 October 1762.

FONTENELLE
King's doctor (medecin), 1748; counciler on the Superior Council, 1757; revoked by order of 1 October 1759; died the same year at Havana returning to France.

FOUBERT
Ensign en pied, 1758; sent back from service. He never went to the colony, having been put in prison at Brest for disorderly conduct (tapage). See the letter of M. de Blenac, commandant of the marine at Brest, of 19 March 1759.

FOUCAULT
Scrivener of the Marine; went to Louisiana in January 1762. Nota: Sieur Foucault carries an order of the King dated 1 January 1762 to carry out the functions of ordonnateur in case Sieur D'Abbadie does not arrive in the colony or dies.

GAMON DE LA ROCHETTE GOURDON
Lieutenant reformé in France, 1747; captain in Louisiana, 1 October 1750.

GARDRAT
Surgeon (chirurgien) - major, 1754.

GARIC
Recorder of the Superior Council, 1 January 1762.

GIRARDEAU, THE CADET
Second lieutenant, 15 October 1752; ensign en pied, 1 July 1759.

GIRARDEAU, THE ELDER
Second lieutenant, 11 June 1750; ensign en pied, 1 February 1754; lieutenant, 1 October 1762.

𝓗

HAZEUR
Ensign, 1732; lieutenant, 1736; Captain, 1746. He died in December, 1758.

HARPAIN DE LA GAUTRAYE
Cadet at Rochfort; ensign in Louisiana; lientenant, 1 October 1740; captain, 1 February 1754; Chevalier de St. Louis, 30 June 1775. He died at Hotel Dieu of Angers, 15 May 1776. The baptism certificate is attached to the dossier on letter L no. 82.

HEUGON DESDEMAINE
Second lieutenant, 1 June 1746; ensign en pied, 15 October 1752; lieutenant, 1 July 1759; Chevalier de St. Louis, 18 August 1722. He retired 26 October 1762, with a pension of 300 livres from the Royal Treasury, beginning from the first of the said month.

HUREAU de LIVOIS
Lieutenant in the militia batallion of Montgaris, 15 February 1747; an interruption (of service?); lieutenant in Louisiana, 1 July 1751; captain, 1 October 1762.

HUREAU DE LIVOY
Lieutenant in the militia batallion of Montargis, 1747; lieutenant in Louisiana, 1 July 1751; captain, 1 October 1762.

JUZANT
Second lieutenants, 15 October 1752; ensign en pied, 15 May 1762.

KERNION
Councilor, 10 January 1762.

KERNION
Second lieutenant, 1 February 1754; ensign en pied, 1 July 1759.

LA BOUCHERIE FROMENTEAU
Second lieutenant at Isle Royale, 15 April 1750; sub-lieutenant of the company canoniers bombardiers at Isle Royale, 1 April 1755; lieutenant of the second company of the same, 1 February 1758; Went to serve in the same capacity in Louisiana following the choice that Mr. Daubigny, commandant of the marine at Rochefort, made on the dispatch of the Duke de Choiseul, 7 January 1762.

LA FOREST de LAUMONT
Lieutenant of the Grenadiers of the Batallion of St. Maixant, 1746; ensign in Louisiana, 1 October 1750; lieutenant, 1 July 1759. He was drowned in the sinking of the Père de Famille, 17 February 1770, returning to France. The certificate was delivered in 1770.

LA FRESNIERE
Councilor, 1 January 1762.

LA LANDE DALCOURT
Second lieutenant, 15 October 1752; ensign en pied, 1 July 1759.

LA LOIRE
Second lieutenant, 1 October 1762.

LA PERLIERE
Second lieutenant, 1 October 1740; ensign en pied, 1 June 1746; lieutenant, 15 October 1752.

LA PERRIÈRE
Lieutenant in the Regiment of Montboissier; King's Guard, 1749; lieutenant in Louisiana, 1751; went to Santo Domingo, 1 April 1762; and returned to Louisiana in 1763 as captain.

LE BEAU
King's doctor (medecin), by brevet of 8 January 1761, for Botany and research on natural history.

LE BLANC
Lieutenant in the Batallion of Rhodez; ensign in Louisiana, 1 October 1750; lieutenant, 1 July 1759.

LE BOSSU
Served fifteen years in the Regiment of Poitou, and was wounded at the attack of the entrenchment of Chateau Dauphin in 1744; lieutenant in the Regiment of the Dauphine Allemand, 1 August 1747; lieutenant in Louisiana, 1 October 1750; captain, 1 July 1759; Chevalier de St. Louis, 1 January 1773. (There is an) order of 15 September 1769 which accords him in retirement the 800 livres of appointment which he merits as captain and an extraordinary gratuity of 1200 livres.

LE BRUN
Second lieutenant in the Regiment of Alsace; ensign en pied at Isle Royalle, 15 April 1750; ensign en pied at Louisiana, 1 April 1755; lieutenant, 1 July 1759. (He) is (now) captain in the legion of Isle de France.

LE DOUX
Lieutenant in the Regiment of Custine; lieutenant in Louisiana, 1 October 1750; captain, 1 October 1762.

LE DOUX
Lieutenant in the regiment of Custine; lieutenant in Louisiana, 1 October 1750; captain, 1 October 1762.

LE GROS de LA GRANDCOUR
Ensign en pied, 1 February 1758; 200 livres reformé pension, by a decision of 25 January 1770; obtained 100 livres increase.

LE SASSIER
Councilor at Port au Prince; assessor.

LANTAGNAC
Lieutenant reformé, 15 July 1762.

LAVAU TRUDEAU
Ensign in the company of artillary in Louisiana, 15 May 1762.

LOBINOIS
Principal scrivener; dead.

LOPINOT de BEAUPORT
Second lieutenant at Isle Royale, 1 April 1754; ensign en pied of the second company of canoniers bombardiers at Isle Royale, 1 February 1758; Went to serve in the same capacity in Louisiana following the choice that Mr. Daubigny, commandant of the marine at Rochefort, made on the dispatch of the Duke de Choiseul, 7 January 1762. He was given a commission to maintain the rank of captain, 5 November 1769; brevet of major in the troops of the colony, 12 January 1770; 600 livres gratuity.

MACARTY, THE ELDER
Second lieutenant, 15 May 1762.

MAREST de LA TOUR
Second lieutenant, 15 May 1762.

MAREST DE LA TOUR
Retired ensign; lieutenant, 15 February 1736; Captain, 1 October 1741; Chevalier de St. Louis, 1 August 1759.

MIGNOT
Scrivener of the Marine; comptroller of Louisiana by an order of 1 January 1762; went to Guadeloupe.

MONGIN
Second lieutenant, 1 February 1754; ensign en pied, 1 July 1759.

MONIN de CHAMPIGNY
Standard bearer, 1 April 1754; engineer, 1 January 1762; captain, 1 January 1762; in Guyanne, serving in the same capacity, 1 January 1763. Captain in the legion of Isle de France, certified 8 Nivose.

MONIN de VAUCORET
Lieutenant en pied, 1753; captain reformé, 1759; Chevalier de St. Louis, 8 February 1760. He was made lieutenant colonel in the volunteers of Hainault colonel M. de Grandmaison in 1761.

MONSIEUR de KERLEREC de KRASEGANT (sic)
Naval guard, 1720; sub-lieutenant, 1731; lieutenant de vaisseau, 1741; Chevalier de St. Louis, 1746; Ship's Captain, 1751; governor of Louisiana, 1752. (There is a) letter of the king for his recall.

MONSIEUR AUBRY
Lieutenant of the Lyonnais Regiment, 1742; Captain in Louisiana, 18 October 1750; Chevalier de St. Louis. 10 July 1761. Drowned in the sinking of the Père de Famille, Jacqueline, captain, on 17 February 1770, returning to France.

NERMAN
Scrivener, 1 January 1758. He was recalled by an order of 1 January 1762, to serve at Rochefort.

OLIVIER de VEZIN
Grand inspector of highways and arpenter general, 1747.

PAUPULUS
Second lieutenant, 7 October 1733; ensign en pied, 15 October 1736; lieutenant, 1 June, 1746; captain, 15 October 1752; Chevalier de St. Louis, 19 January 1777.

PELLERIN
Second lieutenant, 15 October 1752; ensign en pied 1 July 1759.

PESCHON
Second lieutenant, 1 June 1746; ensign en pied, 11 June 1750; lieutenant, 1 July 1759.

PHILIPPE
Second lieutenant, 1 February 1754; ensign en pied, 1 July 1759.

PIOT de LAUNAY
Councilor, 10 January 1762.

POILLEVÉ
Second lieutenant, 15 May 1762.

POPULUS, THE ELDER
Second lieutenant, 15 May 1762.

RAGUET
Senior member of the council; dead.

RAIMBAULT LA MOËLE
Second lieutenant in Canada, 15 April 1750; ensign en pied in Canada, 15 March 1755; lieutenant in Canada, 1 January 1759; went to Louisiana in the same capacity by an order of 1 January 1762.

RENARD de COUDREAU
Second lieutenant, 15 October 1752; ensign en pied, 1 February 1754; lieutenant of the cannoneers, 1 November 1759.

ROBERT de LA MORANDIÈRE

Expectative of second lieutenant, 25 March 1748; second lieutenant, 11 June 1750; ensign en pied, 1 February 1754; lieutenant, 1 October 1762.

ROULLIN

Lieutenant in the militia batallion of Neufchatel, 1 April 1742; volunteer to the regiment of Orleans dragonson, 1743; second lieutenant in the regiment of Orleans, Infantry, 25 December 1744; lieutenant in the same regiment, 10 June 1745; ensign in Louisiana, 1 October 1750; lieutenant, 1 July 1759; commission to retain the rank of captain in the colonial troops, 11 May 1770; pay of 400 livres, 1770; Chevalier de St. Louis, 18 November 1770.

S

ST. ANGE

Captain reformé, 15 October 1748.

ST. DENIS, THE CADET

Second lieutenant, 15 October 1752; ensign en pied, 1 October 1762.

ST. DENIS, THE ELDER

Second lieutenant, 1 June 1746; ensign en pied, 15 October 1752; lieutenant, 1 July 1759.

SARRAZIN

Lieutenant reformé, 29 November 1762.

SAUSSIER

Second lieutenant, 15 May 1762.

SCIMARS de BELLISLE

Former enseigne en pied; lieutenant, 18 July 1734; aide-major of New Orleans, 14 September 1735; captain, 1 October 1740; major of New Orleans, 15 October 1752; Chevalier de St. Louis, 15 October 1752; now dead. Put in order and dismissed by an order of 1 October 1759, to be returned to France. . . .

T

TIXERAND

Second lieutenant, 15 October 1752; ensign en pied, 1 October 1762.

TIXERANT

Second lieutenant, 15 October 1722 (sic); ensign en pied, 1 October 1762.

TOULON

Cadet a l'Eguillette, 1754; second lieutenant, 15 May 1762.

TRUDEAU

Second lieutenant, 14 September 1735; ensign en pied, 1 October 1740; lieutenant, 1 December 1747; captain, 1 July 1759.

TRUDEAU, THE ELDER

Second lieutenant, 15 May 1762.

##

VALENTIN DES ILLETS

Second lieutenants, 1 January 1762.

VALLETTE

Arpenter, 1 October 1759.

VAUGELADE de GRANDCHAMP
Garde du corps du Roi; captain en second of the hussards in the volunteers of Gantes, 1746; captain in Louisiana, 1 October 1750; Chevalier de St. Louis, 1 July 1770. (There is an) order of 15 September 1769 which grants him in retirement, the 1080 livres of appointments which he merits as captain, with an extraordinary gratuity of 1200 livres.

VEDRINE
Second lieutenant, 15 October 1752; ensign en pied, 1 July 1759.

VILLARS DUBREUIL
Second lieutenant, 1 October 1762.

VILLERÉ
Scrivener-ordinary.

VOISIN
Second lieutenant, 15 October 1736; ensign en pied, 1 June 1746; lieutenant, 15 October 1752; captain, 1 July 1759.

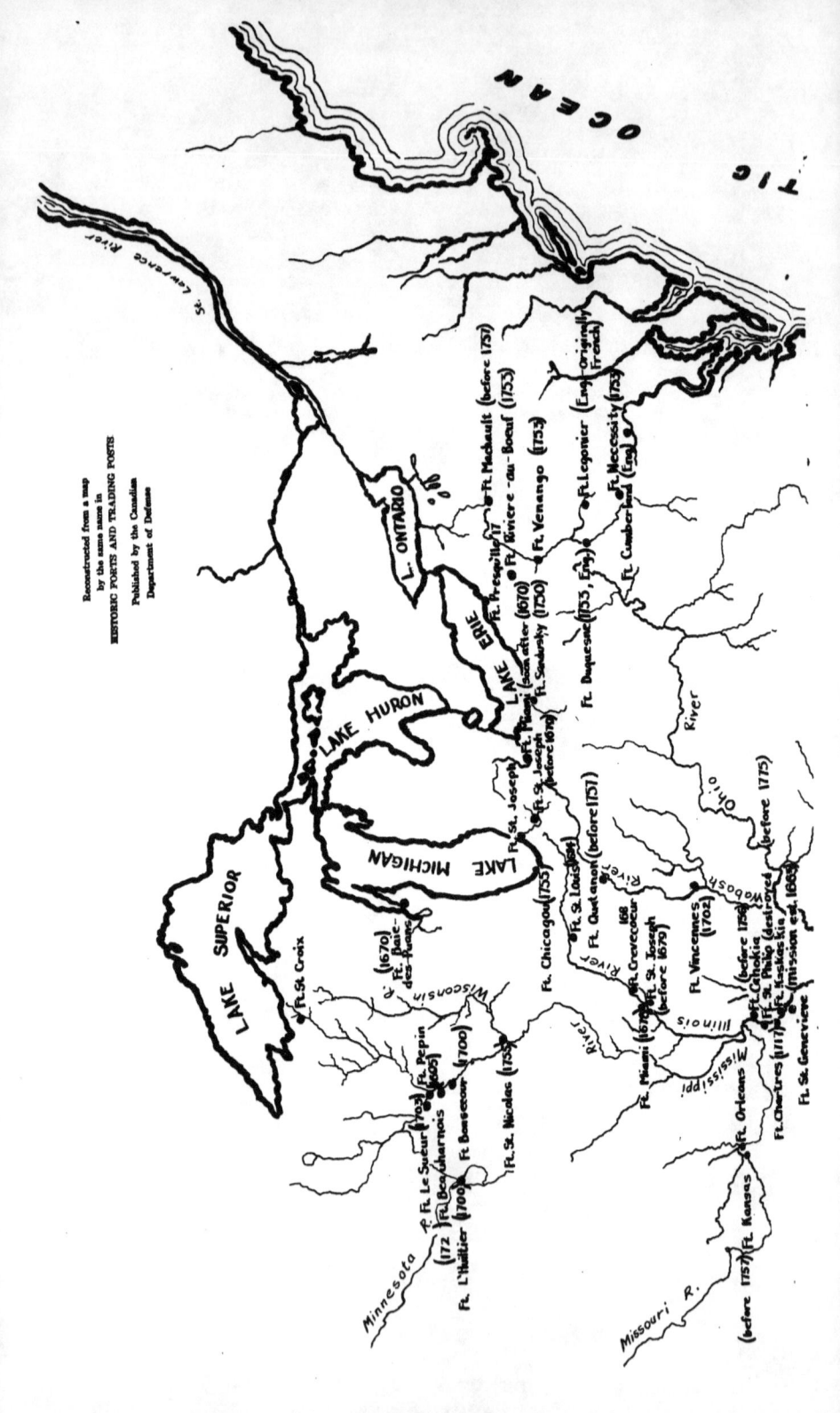

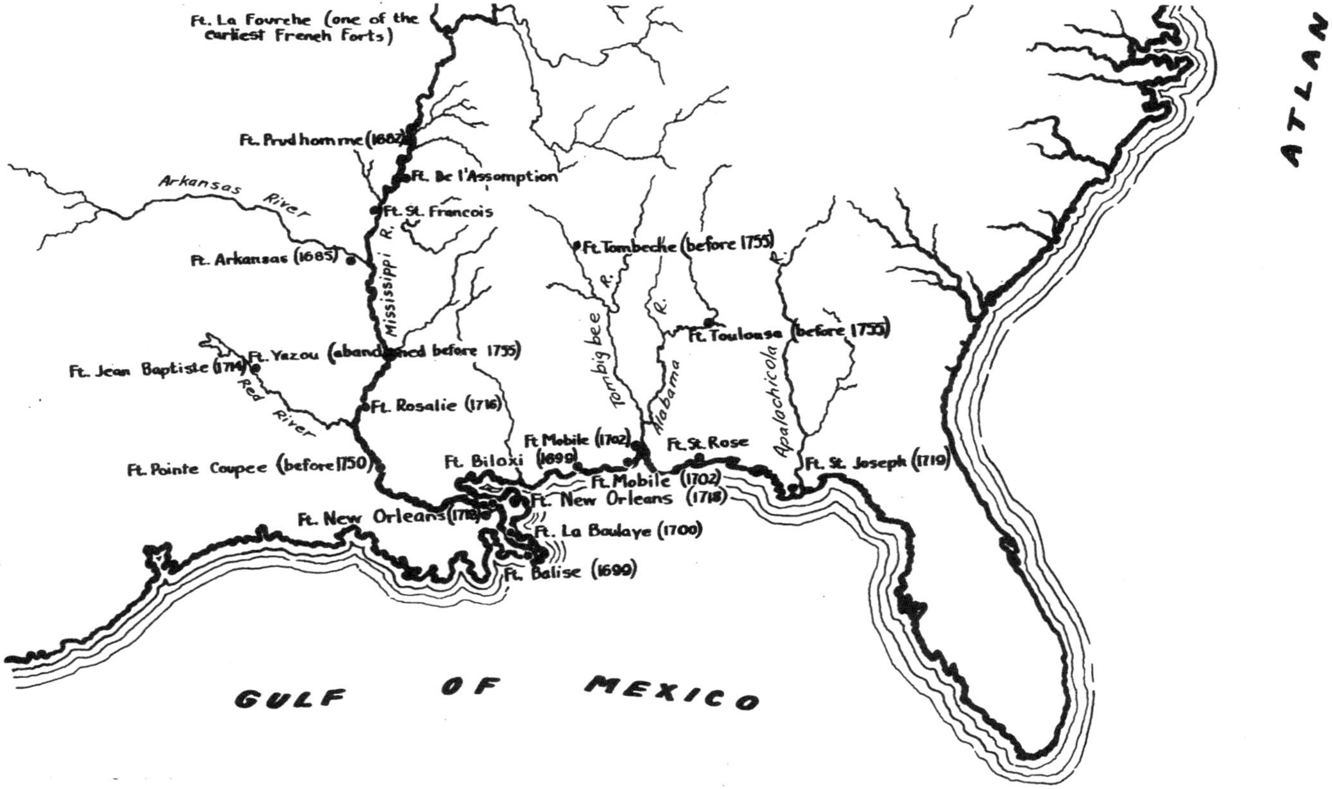
Ft. La Fourche (one of the earliest French Forts)
Ft. Prudhomme (1682)
Ft. De l'Assomption
Ft. St. Francois
Arkansas River
Ft. Arkansas (1685)
Mississippi R.
Ft. Tombeche (before 1755)
Tombigbee R.
Alabama R.
Ft. Toulouse (before 1755)
Apalachicola R.
Ft. Yazou (abandoned before 1755)
Ft. Jean Baptiste (1714)
Red River
Ft. Rosalie (1716)
Ft. Mobile (1702)
Ft. St. Rose
Ft. Biloxi (1699)
Ft. St. Joseph (1719)
Ft. Pointe Coupee (before 1750)
Ft. Mobile (1702)
Ft. New Orleans (1718)
Ft. New Orleans (1718)
Ft. La Boulaye (1700)
Ft. Balise (1699)
ATLAN
GULF OF MEXICO

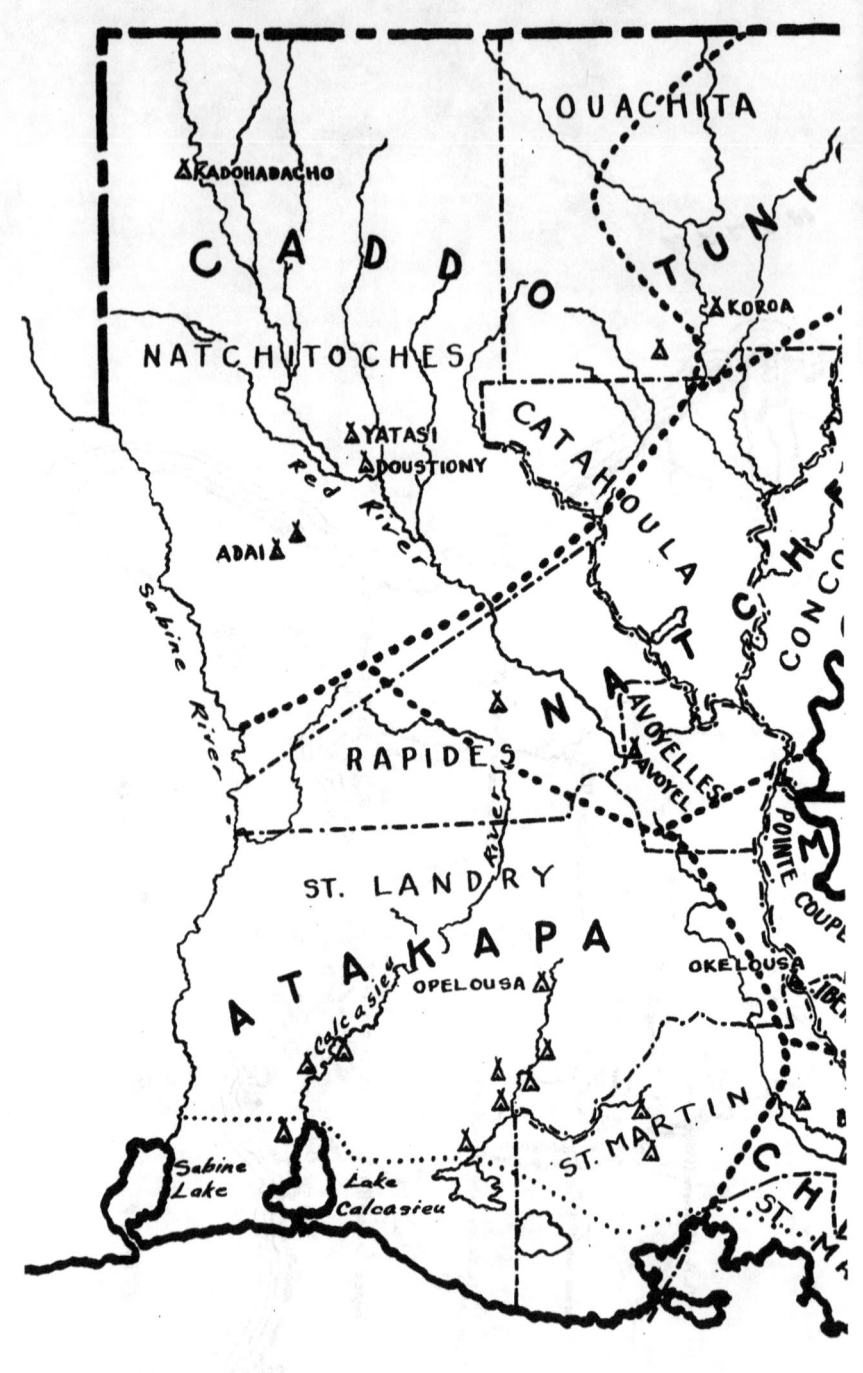

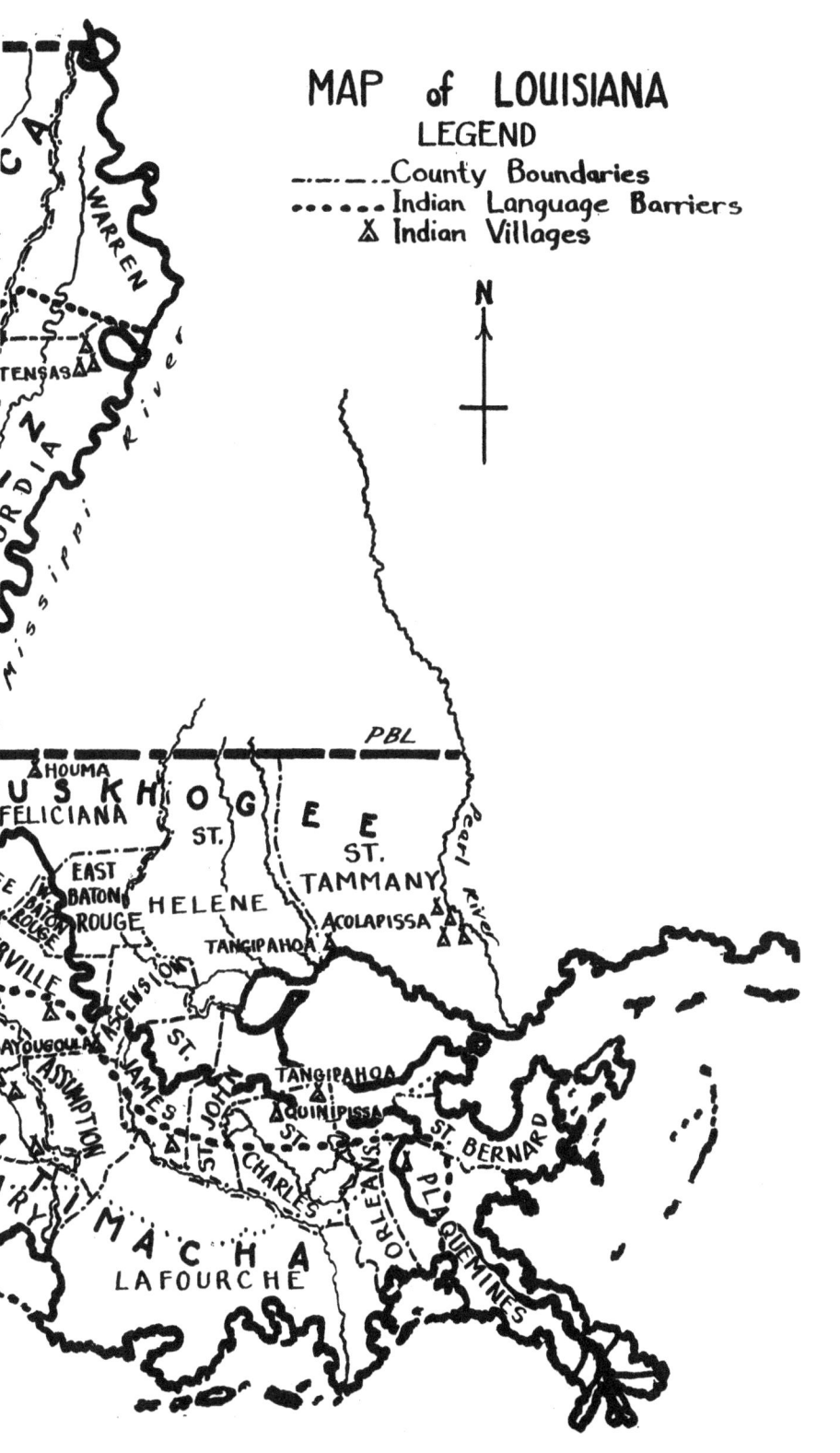

www.ingramcontent.com/pod-product-compliance
Lightning Source LLC
Chambersburg PA
CBHW072147160426
43197CB00012B/2285